"The simplicity and directness of the book really hit those of us who are striving for balance in our lives. Living the balanced 'on-purpose' life requires the kind of structure and encouragement that are provided in this book."
— Steve S. Reinemund, President and CEO, Pizza Hut

"The secret of success is: Do more of what you're good at and less of what you're not good at. That's what *The On-Purpose Person* is all about."
— Stanley C. Olsen, Co-founder, Digital Equipment Corp.; Developer, Black Diamond Ranch

"What a refreshing book! To the point, and with the passion only a true believer can communicate, *The On-Purpose Person* should take its rightful place in every thinking person's bookcase."
— Michael Gerber, CEO, The Michael Gerber Corporation, and author of *The E Myth*

"*The On-Purpose Person* is the book to read before you read *What Color Is Your Parachute?*"
— Connee Sullivan, Vice President of Corporate Finance, Prudential Insurance Company

"I was so excited about *The On-Purpose Person* that I purchased dozens of copies to share with family, friends, business associates, and church members! It works!"
— Roger Stitt, President, RHS Construction Company

"In my psychiatry practice, I see many patients struggling to find themselves. I help them focus on their assets and get moving—much like *The On-Purpose Person* does. The only difference is that I use psychiatric jargon, attach labels, and charge fees. What Kevin is doing, if it were to become well-known, would put me and other psychiatrists like me out of business."
— Walter J. Muller, III, M.D., The Group for Psychiatry, Psychology, and Social Services

"I read *The On-Purpose Person* with interest and excitement. I kept asking myself: Am I an On-Purpose Person?"
—The Reverend Peter Moore, Rector,
Little Trinity Church, Montreal,
and author of *Disarming Secular Gods*

"Many books assert that one must have a goal to be happy and successful. *The On-Purpose Person* is the first one to show me how to determine what my goals should be."
—Thomas P. Page, Attorney at Law,
Mateer, Harbert & Bates, P.A.

"Without a doubt this is the best guide I have seen for creating a meaningful and balanced life plan."
—Malcome E. Hawley, DDS

"*The On-Purpose Person* is a valuable addition to an important and growing literature on effective time management and leadership. McCarthy brings to life and operationalizes powerful ideas that will help all of us make a difference."
—John W. Rosenblum, Dean, The Darden School

"The best tool I've seen for turning good intentions into positive actions. Highly recommended for anybody, but especially for those who need a way to organize unstructured time—like clergy!"
—The Right Reverend William Frey,
Dean, Trinity Episcopal School for Ministry

A MODERN PARABLE

The
ON-PURPOSE
PERSON

MAKING YOUR
LIFE
MAKE SENSE

KEVIN W. MCCARTHY

P.O. Box 35007
Colorado Springs, CO 80935

Library of Congress Catalog Card Number:
        92-61234
ISBN 08910-97058

Cover illustration: Bill Frampton

Printed in the United States of America

   8 9 10 11 12 13 14 15 / 00 99 98 97

CONTENTS

How to Maximize Your Benefit
from This Book   11

DISCOVERY
1.   "Success"   15
2.   A Different Path   23
3.   The On-Purpose Person   27

Step One: A New Beginning
4.   Out of Chaos   33
5.   A Single Step   37
6.   The Tournaments   43
7.   A New Order   53

Step Two: The Plan
8.   Effective and Efficient   57
9.   The Ideal On-Purpose Day   63
10.   Truths   69

Step Three: Simplify
11.   On-Purpose Statements   79
12.   The Seasons of Life   93

TRANSFORMATION
13.   Choices and Risks   101
14.   On-Purpose with Passion   107
15.   The On-Purpose Person in Creation   111
16.   Giving   117
17.   The Gathering   129

THE REWARD
18.   True Success   135

Appendix   139

To my son,
Charles Claiborne McCarthy,
who was born during the writing of this book
on February 21, 1991.
After years of infertility related issues
and wanting to share our lives with a child,
Judith and I were blessed by his arrival—
a miracle even by today's medical standards.

ACKNOWLEDGMENTS

Writing a book is a monumental undertaking. Although the author is on center stage, many people behind the scenes contribute in their own personal, special manner. In a sense, it becomes a group effort. I'd like to thank my cast:

Special thanks to the Reverend Paul Crowell for his many suggestions, which were incorporated into early drafts.

A special tribute to Betty Pratt and Perry Nies, who generously allowed me to model characters in the book after their on-purpose lives.

For their reading of early drafts and encouragement along the way, many thanks to Steve Levée, Jane and Perry Nies, Shirley Pipkin, John Budlong, George Romot, Harry Griffith, Alan Welsh, Denny Johnson, Frank Attwood, Dr. Ron Behner, John Smith, Peter Moore, Roger Stitt, David H. Wilson, my CEO group, Vicky McVay, Murray Fisher, Tom Downs, Walter Walker, and Thayer Bigelow.

Thank you to Bob Smith of American Reprographics in Winter Park, Florida, for your guidance, printing, and binding of my original self-published books. Truly, your service is legendary!

Becky Kaiser provided editing and typing for much of the original manuscript.

My publisher, Piñon Press, has been a tremendous partner in this project. I couldn't handpick a nicer and more professionally competent team. Nancy Burke is consistently a joyful and ready helper. Bruce Nygren shared the vision and possibilities immediately. He is my editorial director, project leader, guide, and friend. His willingness to listen, patience, and sound suggestions led to major improvements in the manuscript.

My parents and brother, Bob, were there for me in the formative years of my life. They encouraged me and allowed me to learn life's lessons. I've never felt more appreciation and love than I do today for the blessings they are in my life.

I want to thank my wife, Judith, from whom I never heard a discouraging word during the term of this writing project. She is my best friend and my love.

Foremost, I want to thank God for the life experiences, giftedness, and inspiration that led to and enabled the writing of this book—his handiwork through me.

How to Maximize Your Benefit from This Book

The following suggestions are offered to enhance your personal development and learning, and to increase the value and enjoyment of your reading experience.

1. Read *The On-Purpose Person* cover to cover. Enjoy the story—it's thought-provoking and reads quickly. You'll receive great tips to get you on your way to becoming an On-Purpose Person. In other words, get the big picture, then go back and develop your On-Purpose Person Program.

2. As you're reading, if you're anxious to get started, you may want to keep a journal of your impressions, thoughts, and insights. Do what works best for you.

3. Keep *The On-Purpose Person* handy for spontaneous review. Some readers keep it in their briefcase or purse and pull it out to read for highly effective and efficient on-purpose minutes while waiting in line at the bank or grocery store, for their next appointment, for their food to arrive, in rush-hour traffic, until the bus comes, and so on. Also, you'll find it helpful to keep it close by your On-Purpose Folder for easy reference.

4. Remember this book. Don't just set it aside

and forget about it. There will be a time in your life—perhaps it's now—when you will invest time in the Program. When you do, read each chapter and follow the Program.

Please don't force yourself or others to embark on the Program simply for the sake of doing it. There's a time and place to delve into *The On-Purpose Person*. When you're ready, you'll know it. Perhaps it will take the form of forty minutes a day for a fortnight. It might be a trip to the beach, a long weekend to the mountains or the cabin, or maybe the last week of the year. Set your own pace for discovery and personal renewal.

5. Each year, repeat the steps outlined in *The On-Purpose Person*. Becoming an On-Purpose Person is like learning any skill—repetition builds proficiency. The Program is absorbed quickly and there are no "right" answers. Move at a comfortable pace. Experience it the first time, and allow your proficiency to improve with practice and repetition. Your happiness, success, and achievements will soar as you learn to be an On-Purpose Person.

6. Encourage others to read the book. Share the experience, and your life will be enhanced.

Read on and have fun . . . On-Purpose!

KEVIN W. MCCARTHY

P.S. If *The On-Purpose Person* touches your life, please let me know. That is a gift you can share with me. Your comments and suggestions are most welcome. My address is on page 144.

DISCOVERY

A purpose is more on-going and gives meaning to our lives. . . . When people have a purpose in life, they enjoy everything they do more!

People go on chasing goals to prove something that doesn't have to be proved: that they're already worthwhile.

"The fastest way to achieve goals," the successful salesperson said, "is to stay on purpose."

Spencer Johnson, M.D., and Larry Wilson
The One-Minute $alesperson

1

"SUCCESS"

▼

*The mass of men lead lives
of quiet desperation.*

Henry David Thoreau

O nce there was a very successful person.

In fact, he was more than successful: his life had meaning and purpose. He knew he was using his time on earth to make a significant difference in other people's lives. He had come to terms with himself; he accepted his strengths as well as his weaknesses. He tried hard to be a better person. He understood, appreciated, and loved many people. People were drawn to him—whether family, friends, business associates, or casual acquaintances.

But it hadn't always been that way.

He still carried the memories of those years of frustration when his life had no purpose or foundation. Back then, "living" was just going through the motions, stretched out along a string of days spent reacting to circumstances and people who called the shots for him. He was not in control of his life.

That was many years ago. Things were different now. He had learned a great deal since then. And what he had learned he put into practice—on-purpose.

LEARNING TO PERFORM

As a boy, he had not felt special. He was often an awkward and embarrassed kid. When he got to junior and senior high school, he overcame his awkwardness by blending in with friends. It was easier and more acceptable to go along with the crowd. He never got into any real trouble. He figured out how to stay on good terms with most people. All in all, life was pretty good then, at home and at school.

As a college student, he sharpened his ability

to sense what others wanted. He knew the majority rules in a democracy—so the thing to do was become part of the majority. It was an easy strategy: just wait and see, and then do as others did.

His strategy worked. He was popular and a student government leader. It was a rush to have "Big Man on Campus" status.

He found success came easily. All he did was find out what others wanted and then act accordingly. He talked to enough people to keep up on the majority opinion, so he continued to be popular and respected among the student body, faculty, and school administration alike.

It seemed that he had discovered a secret to success.

Or had he?

CLIMBING THE LADDER

He was almost done with school now. College life had been great. True, his grades had slipped a little and his girlfriend was more demanding. His relationship with his parents was strained, too. And his brother was a nuisance. But so what?—he could deal with that later when he had more time. After all, he was good at smoothing things over.

He graduated and took his choice of several job offers. He got on board with a large, well-respected company. His friends were getting married, so he and his girlfriend tied the knot. It was a good move for his career, he figured.

It wasn't long before he was promoted to a management position. He bought a new car, and a nice house in the suburbs. He and his wife were expecting a child. His star was on the rise.

As a company manager, each step of his climb to power and responsibility was hard-earned. His ability to detect and deliver on other people's expectations was masterful. His boss continued giving him good reviews and raises, and he was popular with those who reported to him.

Things were going well on other fronts, too. His parents were proud of him. His wife and children were well cared for. They moved into a bigger house in a nicer, more expensive neighborhood. His kids began attending a private school. He became an active volunteer with the United Way.

His climb up the ladder was taking him to the top. He had the corporate title and the financial rewards to show for it.

"Success"—he had it all.

Or did he?

WHEN IT STARTED TO COME APART

He worked hard to maintain his success. But somewhere along the way, the shining star of success began to lose its luster.

At work, challenges and opportunities were turning into frustrations and disappointments. He was just going through the motions. Yet he couldn't quit his job because his family counted on him to provide for them. Worse still, their financial situation was out of control. The more money he made, the more he and his family wanted, and the more they spent.

Deep inside he wondered, *What's become of*

my dreams? He became increasingly resentful and impatient with everything and everybody. Afraid he would explode from frustration and say things he might later regret, he avoided personal conversations and increasingly withdrew from others.

On the outside he still looked the picture of success. But on the inside he was slowly dying. He couldn't keep it all together anymore. There just wasn't enough time in the day to do everything he was supposed to do, even though he worked harder and longer. He got up earlier and went to bed later. He was always late to his kids' after-school activities — if he got there at all. His parents grew increasingly dependent on him, and their expectations weighed heavily on him.

The company expected him to be active in the community. He felt caught in the middle when he was asked to head the charity drive at the local civic club. Where was he going to find the time?

Things at home weren't any better either. Although he wasn't exactly sure when the shift had taken place, his wife's encouragement had turned into nagging. Her conversation was simply irritating static. He responded by tuning her out as background noise or engaging her in yet another inconclusive argument climaxed by his storming out of the room. They stopped speaking to each other.

The children — they were growing up so quickly! He hardly knew or even talked with them. Communication seemed limited to turf battles for TV channels, complaints about house rules, endless requests for money for this, that, and the next thing. . . .

What's happening to me? he thought. *Where did things go wrong?*

But there were no answers for his questions.

TRYING TO MAKE SENSE OF IT ALL

He started daydreaming about how to start his life all over again. He could get a new job, perhaps move to a new town—only this time he wouldn't become so involved. Maybe he should divorce his wife so he could get rid of his growing marital problems.

In despair, he even considered suicide as a possible way out. *He* couldn't do that. Everyone expected better from him.

After all, he thought, *what would God think about suicide?* Then it hit him. *Wait a minute— where is God in all of this? It feels like even he's abandoned me.*

Loneliness washed over him in waves. No one could understand his situation. How much longer could he keep up this facade of success before it fell apart to expose the reality underneath? He was living an unfulfilled, meaningless life. A life without purpose.

But how to get back in touch with what was important to him? He didn't want to let anyone down. He wasn't even sure he knew anymore what he wanted out of life.

These thoughts increased the pressure all the more. He was running out of time—his balancing act had become too risky and strenuous to maintain. He was holding his life together by an ever-so-frayed string. But it wasn't really *his* life. He was out of control, out of touch with his dreams.

He had no way out, and it showed. He was over-weight, frustrated with his job, anxious about his children, and distant from his wife. He escaped by drinking more and more.

People around him couldn't comprehend that in the midst of his "success" he was scared to death and miserably unhappy. His life seemed to be one big snarl of conflicts, which left him feeling compromised and hollow.

On a rare occasion he confided his anxiety and fear to a friend. But all he got back was, "Don't worry—you've got it made! You're just going through a phase of life. It'll pass."

However well-intended, those words of "encouragement" left him feeling more alone and confused than ever. It was like he was lost at sea, crying out for help, but the occasional passing boaters told him he didn't have a problem. Misguided platitudes only heightened his desperation. He grew increasingly unwilling to risk reaching out for help.

This can't be all there is to life! he exclaimed to himself. *There must be more. There must be a way out of this dead end, a way to balance it all, a way to find meaning and significance. There must be a purpose for my life.*

Something clicked just then. *Purpose.* The word snapped him to attention. He'd heard about a remarkable man—someone had called him an "On-Purpose Person." Who was this guy? Oh yes . . . a college professor, supposedly accessible to people.

The man decided to call the professor. Something in his life *had* to change. He needed help.

What did he have to lose?

2

A Different Path

▼

Darest thou, now O soul,
Walk out with me toward
the unknown region
Where neither ground is
for the feet nor any path
to follow?

Walt Whitman

H is call to the college professor was answered on the first ring.

"Hello-o!" said an enthusiastic and somewhat whimsical voice. "What is the purpose of your call?"

The man sensed already why this professor was called an On-Purpose Person. "I'm not quite sure why I'm calling," he responded. "You're known as an On-Purpose Person, and I thought — well — maybe you could help me."

"Tell me more." The professor's voice changed. "Please, tell me more," he repeated in a genuine tone. The man had a sudden, immediate sensation that he was the only person in the world the professor knew or cared about.

"I'm considered to be successful," he started in. "In fact, quite successful. I'm a fast-tracker. I have a nice house in the suburbs, two new cars, a couple of kids. . . ." The tape was rolling. It was his "good guy" speech — the one he'd perfected for introducing himself at cocktail parties, trade shows, and clubs.

"Again, sir. What is the purpose of your call?" interrupted the professor. This time his voice was forceful. It indicated that the man had better make his point — soon. "Why did you call, if you're so successful?"

The professor wasn't buying his story. "Actually, I'm not really that successful," he retreated. "I've always been able to meet other people's expectations, but for some reason it's getting harder and harder, and I don't know how much longer I can keep it up. Frankly, I'm desperate and I need help.

I can't find any meaning or significance for my life. I'm so out of touch, so hollow. I'm losing my integrity. Along the way, I seem to have lost the real me."

He paused, but the professor said nothing.

"I'm ready to make changes, but I don't know where or how to start. I was hoping you could help me. I'd like to make an appointment to see you."

"Your words are familiar," said the professor. "Are you interested in discovering a different path to travel?"

"Yes!" he exclaimed.

"May I share with you the different path and process of an On-Purpose Person?"

"Yes, absolutely."

"Are you available to visit me in my office tomorrow from three to three-thirty?" asked the professor.

"Yes, I want to hear what you have to say," he replied. "I'll be there."

As he hung up the phone he thought, *I wonder what an On-Purpose Person is all about? It'll be interesting to hear what this professor has to say. Could he possibly show the way to a meaningful life?*

3

THE ON-PURPOSE PERSON

▼

Enter to grow in wisdom.
Depart better to serve
thy country and mankind.

Charles William Eliot
(Inscription on the
1890 Gate to Harvard Yard)

Amid the laughter and chatter of students in the hallway, the man found the open door of the professor's office. He knocked on the door frame.

A trim man with engaging eyes turned in his chair and looked toward him. With an inviting wave of his hand and a big smile, he said, "Come on in."

The man took notice of the professor. He projected a sense of friendliness, caring, and peace. The man felt at ease. The professor had a genuineness about him . . . the feel of a person with a sincere quality and compassion.

He entered the office, immediately noticing an award on the wall directly in front of him for the outstanding professor in the university as elected by students and faculty. He scanned the room quickly and took in its contents: family pictures adorning the desk . . . several tennis rackets stacked neatly in a corner.

Then he met the friendly and inquiring gaze of the professor. *No wonder he's so popular with the students,* the man thought to himself. *He's so genuine—a person of sincerity and compassion.*

"Welcome!" exclaimed the professor. They shook hands and then sat down in a small grouping of chairs away from the desk.

They chatted easily, exchanging bits of background information. After a few minutes the professor asked, "So, what is the purpose of your visit?"

The man was feeling quite comfortable with the professor. He had expected the professor might start with this question. After all, he was accomplished at knowing other people's expectations.

"I've thought about that question since my telephone call yesterday. The bottom line is, my life is without meaning and significance. I've tried goal-setting, seminars, lectures, books, tapes, everything. I should be happy. After all, I've accomplished quite a lot and accumulated reasonable wealth. I'm lucky to have a wife and two children. Most people envy what I have. I'm successful, but it doesn't feel right."

He was aware of the professor's steady, uninterrupted gaze.

"I don't know how to get myself back together again," he went on. "I seem to be possessed by my possessions. My work serves no purpose. My marriage is mere coexistence. My family is like a group of strangers to me. I'm detached from them, and for that matter from everybody else as well. I'm lost and alone. And I'm hurting. I'm hurting bad—bone-deep."

The professor leaned forward, touched the man reassuringly on the forearm, and smiled. Then he sank back into his stuffed chair, looked the man straight in the eye, and said with a chuckle, "Where you are in your life is just perfect! You see, we're all On-Purpose Persons—in creation!"

Anger surged up in him. "You're disrespectful!" he blurted out. "I come in here baring my soul to you, and you—you *laugh!* How dare you?! That's outrageous. Just tell me what this On-Purpose Person stuff is all about, and I'll be on my way."

"Young man, I'm not laughing at you," the professor reassured him. "Thank you for being so open with me. I have great respect for what you just shared with me. I'm laughing at *myself*. You remind me of the way I was at one time in my life. Let me share with you my story of becoming an On-Purpose Person."

He calmed down and nodded his approval.

The professor pointed to a framed picture on the wall. "Do you see this draw-ing of an electrical switch?" he asked, speaking calmly now. "The light switch turned on is the symbol of an On-Purpose Person. It's a reminder that we are either off-or on-purpose— nothing in between. Every time you use a light switch, think to yourself, *Am I off- or am I on-pur-pose?* And then correct or con-gratulate yourself accordingly."

"Purpose is energy," the professor went on. "It's the single most motivating force there is. Discover your purpose, be on-purpose, and you will have a life filled with meaning and significance. We need to be doing and living on-purpose."

"C'mon, professor," the man challenged, "that's easier said than done. Life isn't that simple."

"Yes, it *is* that simple. Living it out," the professor said smiling, "now there's the hard part. Being on-purpose requires discipline and a sustained effort. Many people choose to slide through life. Consider the result—being off-purpose. Isn't that where you find yourself today?"

The words stung. The professor was right. What he'd been doing clearly wasn't working. He needed to establish a new design for his life. The purpose-lessness of his life was evident. Despite his accomplishments, he was lost and out of control. He felt empty.

He thought about a guy at work—a real shark. Sometimes they competed. The shark always seemed to win. This guy would withdraw, protect turf, and then lash out angrily. What if they were both facing similar circumstances and problems, but just reacting differently? A sense of meaninglessness can make a person bitter. He felt a small surge of compassion for his peer.

"Professor," he asked, "what *is* my purpose?"

"Oh!" exclaimed the other, laughing again. "There you go, looking for others to define your purpose. It won't work! Others can help you by affirming what you ask them, by providing you with feedback so that you can better understand yourself. But, it's still 100 percent *your* responsibility to discover your purpose. Anything less is just people-pleasing. That's the pattern that got you here in the first place. Remember, I promised to show you an alternate route, not the destination. I never said it would be easy."

"Well then, how do I get started?"

The professor smiled with delight. Here was his favorite kind of student—a motivated person searching for purpose.

"Why are you so happy?" the man inquired. "I'm a total stranger. I tell you my life is in a shambles, and I need your help. Yet you seem to enjoy this. Why? What's in it for you?"

"Helping you become an On-Purpose Person is on-purpose for me," responded the professor. "And I'm happiest when I'm on-purpose."

The man picked up on the comment. "You know,

there've been times in my life when I've been, in your terms, on-purpose, and I knew it. There was a sense of sheer pleasure, regardless of the drudgery or ease of what I was doing. Energy and life flowed. I was working on something worthwhile. It was a peak experience."

"That's it!" cried the professor. "We *all* have those experiences throughout our lives. For most folks they're random occurrences. On-Purpose Persons are more intentional, so we more frequently enjoy peak experiences. Let's just say we have higher batting averages."

The man was starting to get a taste of what it meant to be an On-Purpose Person. "Okay, professor, you've got my attention. Tell me more about how I can become an On-Purpose Person."

"Young man," said the professor, "here's how you get started on the path of creating a meaningful and balanced life leading to greater and genuine happiness, success, and achievement—the path to becoming an On-Purpose Person."

Step One: A New Beginning

---| **4** |---

OUT OF CHAOS

▼

*The man without a purpose is
like a ship without a rudder —
a waif, a nothing,
a no man.
Have a purpose in life,
and, having it,
throw such strength of mind
and muscle into your work
as God has given you.*

Thomas Carlyle (1795–1881)

The professor rose from his chair and walked behind his walnut desk. He reached into a drawer, pulled out a yellow writing pad and two pens, and handed a pen and eight sheets of paper to the young man. Then, for the first time, the professor sat down at his desk.

"While I'm going through my Rolodex," he said, "I want you to write *want list* across the top of each page. Then on each sheet write a single category, which represents an aspect of your life. On-Purpose Persons call these our life accounts — *accounts*, for short. Here are eight suggested account names:

- Physical/Health/Recreational
- Financial/Material
- Family
- Vocational/Career
- Social/Community
- Spiritual
- Mental/Intellectual
- Other

Two minutes later the man announced, "Professor, I'm finished!"

"Good," replied the professor. "Here's a list of names and phone numbers. Notice that each person is numbered. Call them in the order I've numbered them. Visit with each of them. They are your guides in your search for self-discovery. You are not alone. On each visit take your want list and the other papers you'll accumulate. Eventually they will become your On-Purpose Person's Folder.

"Listen to these On-Purpose Persons, do as they

ask, keep an open mind and a prayerful spirit, and you will be on the path to becoming an On-Purpose Person. I'm the last name on the list. I'll look forward to seeing you again soon."

As the professor placed his arm around the young man's shoulder and walked him to the door, he said, "You are on the threshold of one of the most exciting journeys you will ever take. It is up to you to persevere. The discovery of your purpose will be as high or as low a priority as you want it to be. See it through. It won't be easy. In fact, it may be painful at times. But it's for a good purpose—finding your reason for being—your purpose."

The man shook the professor's hand and thanked him. He picked up his eight sheets of paper with the named accounts and the list of names and telephone numbers. He had met his first On-Purpose Person. He walked through the door, beginning the path to his lifetime adventure.

5

A SINGLE STEP

▼

*A journey of a thousand miles
must begin with a single step.*

Lao-tzu (604–531 BC)

He dialed the first number on the professor's list, curious about who would answer. He was surprised by a youthful-sounding "Hello!"

"Hello," he said. "The professor gave me your name and number."

"Oh, yes. He said you would be calling. I've been looking forward to talking with you. So, what's the purpose of your call?"

He expected that question might be coming. "The purpose of my call is to obtain your guidance in becoming an On-Purpose Person," he replied.

"Great! Would you like to get together tomorrow morning? It's Saturday, so I don't have classes."

"Fine," he answered. "Where can we meet?"

"How about coming by my house around 10:00? My mom and dad will be here then."

"Your parents' house?" He quipped, "How old are you?"

"Old enough to be an On-Purpose Person—in creation, that is. I'm a senior in high school. Next fall, I'm on my way to college, thanks to others who shared with me what it means to be an On-Purpose Person. The professor says you're never too young or too old to start learning and applying the concepts.

"Two years ago," she continued, "I was hanging out with the wrong crowd—doing whatever they were doing. I figured I had plenty of time, so I was in no hurry to change. I did drugs a little and drank a lot. My relationship with my parents was lousy. I was lonely, scared, and unhappy. I tried to escape."

"So how did you find out about becoming an On-Purpose Person?" the man asked.

"My school counselor is an On-Purpose Person. She introduced me to the professor and others. She encouraged me to talk with them. Being an On-Purpose Person makes a positive difference in my life."

"Thanks for sharing that with me," he responded. "I'm looking forward to meeting you. I'll see you tomorrow morning." He was impressed, but remained skeptical. *What could a teenager teach him?*

▼ ▼ ▼

A large man bent over a clump of weeds and gave them a tug. The roots were exposed in an instant. With a flick of his wrist, the weeds flew through the air and landed in a bucket about twenty feet away. Raising a fist above his head, he whooped, "Two points."

"Great shot!" the man cheered and clapped.

The large man turned and acknowledged his fan, "Thank you, thank you. You must be here to see my daughter. The professor told me about you. Go on up to the front door," he pointed. "She's expecting you."

The man rang the doorbell. A girl was visible through the glass door. As she approached, he noticed her youthful, energetic, and confident stride. It was hard to believe this together-looking young girl had ever had such problems.

"I see you met my dad." They both smiled. After a little get-acquainted chatter she asked, "Did you bring your papers with you for your want list?"

"Excuse me—my *what?*"

"Your *want list.* You know, the sheets of paper with the headings."

"Oh—those. Yes, I did."

"Great. Let's get started! It's fun," she said with excitement. "I remember my first want list. I couldn't stop. I just kept on writing. That's the way to do it, though—just keep writing."

"Uh, keep writing what? And why do you and the professor call it your want list?"

"On-Purpose Persons have all kinds of wants, needs, and desires," she answered, "like everyone else. We also have problems, pains, and failures. But the difference is how On-Purpose Persons organize our needs and our response to situations. We are intentional about our lives—we have a purpose.

"Your want list is the first step of that process. It's a comprehensive inventory of what you want, broken down into five to eight primary accounts of your life. Eight is the limit of what's reasonable and manageable. Consolidate accounts if you can; fewer is better. The headings are simply reminders, an aid. It's really the process that's important."

"So, how do I get started on my want list?"

"Begin by getting settled in a place where you can be uninterrupted for a while. Quiet your thoughts and focus on your wants. Next, write down every imaginable want. Let them flow freely—no matter how outrageous they may seem, write them all down. The accounts are for simplifying things later on. Right now, it's important to keep the stream of wants flowing out of your mind and onto the want list. Write as long as you can, then put the list down for a while. I promise you'll pick it up again and again."

She broke into a smile. "It's so much fun just to let your imagination run with it. Dream! Don't worry about how crazy your wants may seem. Like the commercial says: Just Do It!

"You're the only one who ever sees your want list. It's your private playground. Do you understand?"

"Let me make sure," he answered. "I'm to take my eight sheets of paper with a single heading atop each sheet and then just start writing whatever wants come to my mind. Of course, under each heading I'm supposed to put related wants, right?"

"That's right."

"For example, if I want to earn, say, a hundred-twenty thousand dollars next year and to own a silver Buick Park Avenue with a black interior, then this would go under the heading Material/Financial?"

"That's right," she encouraged. "Be specific as you write out your want list. After all, you might as well have fun in living color! And if it's a *core want*, you'll get it."

"So if I want to lose fifteen pounds, I'd put that under" — he quickly flipped through his want list headings — "Physical/Health/Recreational, right?"

"Right!" she said. "It's critical to get your thoughts on paper, fast. If you get hung up trying to decide which category to put a want under, just write it down *somewhere*. You can sort it out later. Keep the stream of thoughts flowing."

"Is there any way I should lay out my wants, other than with the headings for each account?"

"Oh, I'm glad you asked. You reminded me of an important pattern to use as you enter your wants in each account. Within an account alternate writing your wants from the top to the bottom of the page. As your account fills up, your wants will converge at the middle of the page. Later on this is helpful."

"In other words, I place the first want at the top of my page, the second one at the bottom of the page. The third want is at the top, right below the first want. The fourth want is at the bottom of the page, above the second want . . . top, bottom — top, bottom."

"That's right!" she nodded. "Any more questions?"

"And if I run out of space under a heading, may I use more paper?" he asked.

"Yes — bravo!" she cheered. "I like your style. Remember, every want qualifies. It's the process that's important, not the mechanics. Keep your mind running and your pen moving," she added.

"Wow! I can see how this can be fun," the man exclaimed. "I've lost touch with my dreams. This is a great way to get back in touch with what I want out of life. I'm excited!"

He paused, then said, "So what's the next step?"

"One step at a time," she cautioned, "although I applaud your enthusiasm. After you finish your want list, call the next person on the list of names the professor gave you. And remember, this is both fun and serious business. Eventually you'll achieve many of your wants. It's worked for me," she concluded.

"It's been a joy to meet you!" he exclaimed. "You're a wonderful person. Thanks for teaching me a method to get back to my dreams. I think you have a great future ahead of you," he predicted.

"Thank *you*!" she replied. "I know you will discover your purpose."

Shaking hands, they exchanged goodbyes. He could hardly wait to get started on filling out his want list.

---6---

THE TOURNAMENTS

▼

Life does not give itself
to one who tries to keep
all its advantages at once.
I have often thought
morality may perhaps consist
solely in the courage
of making a choice.

Leon Blum (1872–1950)
On Marriage

His hand aching with writer's cramp, he finally laid down his pen. He had put all his wants down on paper. He had at least ten wants under each category—and for one category alone he had filled two sheets of paper!

His second call was to a "B. P. Rose." The name had a familiar ring to it, but he couldn't place it. He dialed the number. After two rings, a woman answered the telephone.

"Hello!"

"Hello! I'm calling for B. P. Rose."

"This is she!"

"Hi, the professor gave me your name." He was ready this time. "The purpose of my call is to ask your assistance in becoming an On-Purpose Person."

"Great! I've been expecting your call. I'm playing tennis tomorrow morning at the public courts in South Park. Would you like to come by after I finish, say around eleven?"

"I'll see you then," he said.

Then he remembered why the name "B. P. Rose" was familiar. She was a tennis champion—a former top-ten player in the world, although she had never achieved the number-one ranking. Later on in age-group competition she had become the top-ranked player and reigned as champion nearly every year for the past twenty-seven years. She had more national championship titles than she was years old!

ENTERING THE COMPETITION

A tanned woman with a wide smile extended her hand to greet him. "Hi! My friends call me Betty.

Thanks for meeting me here at the tennis courts."

"I came by early to watch you train and play. You're remarkable. I see how you stay in competitive form and condition," he commented.

"My tennis is one of my core wants," she stated matter-of-factly. "It's part of what makes me an On-Purpose Person."

"Whatever it is, it sure seems to be working!" he exclaimed.

"Thank you! Our mutual friend, the professor, told me you would be calling. Did you bring your want list?" she asked.

Clutching his handful of pages, he proudly raised them over his head and stated, "Definitely! It was quite an experience. I started very fast. Eventually, I seemed to run out of wants. Then it became more challenging, and I discovered I was going deeper within myself. My wants became, well, less superfical and more centered around my feelings and emotions."

"That's typical and healthy," she affirmed.

"So what's my next step?" he asked.

"Time to compete," she said brightly.

"Hey, wait a minute!" he protested. "I saw you playing. *I* can't play *you*. And besides—I'm not dressed for it, I'm not wearing tennis shoes, I don't have a racquet. . . ."

"Not tennis!" she interrupted, laughing. "I'm talking about those papers you're holding. As you can imagine, every want on your want list competes for your resources, time, energy, and talent. You need a simple system for discerning what's really a priority. That way you can be free to let go of less important wants and commit yourself to the more important ones. Finally, the system must be flexible enough to incorporate the new challenges and opportunities that come your way every day.

"So we have tournaments," she explained. "Once a year I have a major tournament. I get away by myself, create a new want list in every life account, and I run my tournament. It gives me my annual refocus on my purpose. After that, throughout the year, I run mini-tournaments. You'll see what I mean."

It sounded like a good idea to him. "How does it work?" he asked.

"Well, to start," she began, "have a tournament with your wants—actually, two tournaments. First the *qualifiers*, then the *main draw*. Let me show you," she said, motioning toward a large board mounted nearby. "Come here. I'll show you a draw-sheet format."

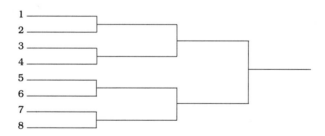

She pointed to the board, which was filled with blank lines. "This is a blank draw-sheet for a tennis tournament with eight participants. The draw-sheet format is used for all kinds of competition—spelling bees, the Super Bowl playoffs, the Final Four. Get the idea?"

"Sure, I recognize it."

"Pull out your want list. For the first category, sequentially number each want all the way down the want list."

He did as she instructed.

"Finished? Great! Now, if you had to choose between want number one and want number two, which would you choose?"

"I guess, uh, number one."

"Now create your own draw sheet. Advance number one to the next round by writing it down in the space to the right that's between numbers one and two. Now, choose between numbers three and four."

"Uh, number four."

"Okay, put number four in the next round. Continue through the entire account, making these decisions in pairs for however many wants you listed. If you don't have an even number of wants, simply advance the leftover want to the next round. That's called a bye."

It seemed simple enough. The sense of organization and accomplishment was gratifying.

"Compete in the next round," Betty continued. "In your case it's now number one versus number four. Write down the winner in the next round."

Something in him started to object. "Wait a minute," he broke in. "I just spent lots of time writing out my want list. Now you're telling me to start eliminating wants."

"Right—partially," she answered. "I understand your concern. Have faith with me at this step. You'll understand in just a minute. You just ran a tournament with the first four wants in one account. You narrowed your selection to one, and only one. Now, tell me how you made your decisions."

"Well," he began, "between one and two, I would give up two in order to get one. Number two was just not as important to me.

"With three and four," he went on, "I realized that if I had four, I would have three as well—so I was better off with four. That made the selection easy.

"Finally," he said, "with number one versus number four, I decided that want number four had more meaning to me than want number one, so I selected number four."

"And how do you feel," she queried, "about leaving behind numbers one, two, and three for the moment?"

"Well, I'm a little disappointed," he admitted, "but I feel fine because number four is the most meaningful."

A little light went on inside him. "Hey, that works!" he exclaimed. "I brought my most meaningful want to the forefront of the other competing wants."

"Right!" she confirmed. "And you haven't eliminated the other wants, because they're still there. They're just postponed for the time being as lower priorities."

"I see," he reflected. "A tournament doesn't need to be just an annual event—it's a tool for everyday use. Hmm . . . say a job offer comes my way. I could incorporate the offer into my want list in the financial and vocational categories. Then I can run a quick tournament and—bingo—I know where I stand. My annual tournament becomes a benchmark for comparison."

"You've got the idea," she encouraged him. "Now that you understand the tournament technique, go through all eight accounts, want by want, using the draw-sheet format to assist you in rank-ordering your selections."

"What if I can't decide between two choices?"

"You have to choose," she stated. Then she asked, "What do you think will produce the best results?"

"I guess going with my first instinct is probably best. It's like taking a true-false test."

"Right again! You're quite good at this. I think you'll be a champion On-Purpose Person in no time," she praised.

Wow! he thought, *that's a compliment from a real champion.* He blushed. "Thank you."

"Come get me when you're finished with the tournament for each of your accounts. In the meantime, I'll be practicing serves on court eight," she pointed, "over there."

PROGRESSING TO THE MAIN DRAW

Want by want, pair by pair, round by round, he went through each account. It was exciting, because he had no clue as to the outcome. At times it was challenging and took some tough decision-making, but he proceeded steadily and finished a short time later. He walked over to court eight where Betty was practicing.

Betty reached deep into the ball hopper for the last tennis ball. She tossed it in the air where it hung momentarily, and with a graceful motion struck it firmly into the corner of the service box. "Ace! Great serve!" he called to her.

She turned and smiled at him.

"I've finished my tournament," he said. "The results are in!"

"Super," she responded. "Your timing is terrific. Would you mind helping me pick up tennis balls while we talk?"

"Happy to," he replied.

"How many wants do you have left?" she asked as they headed across to the other side of the court.

"Eight. One from each account."

"Right. These are your *core wants*. Do you understand why?"

"Let me try!" he said eagerly. "These eight wants represent the most meaningful or highest priority wants for the various areas in my life. The other wants still exist, but these eight are the respective number ones. By focusing my resources on these, will I become an On-Purpose Person?"

"Not so fast," she answered. "That's pretty good. There's more, though. You just held the qualifying tournament. Now you have to run the main draw."

"The main draw?" he inquired.

"What do you think you'll do with the eight core wants?" she asked him.

"Oh-h-h, I see! Run a tournament—the main draw!" he exclaimed.

"Right. Once again, go with your instincts, yet be patient and thoughtful. Think it through. These may be some hard-fought matches— five-setters, in tennis terms."

She smiled and added, "Thanks for your help in

picking up the tennis balls. That part is why I dread practicing my serve. Yet it's a necessary part of my being an On-Purpose Person. After I determined my core wants, I knew the importance in my life of being a champion. The Program cleared away the clutter by helping me focus my energy on my core wants. I dedicated myself to them. Eventually, I became the number-one-ranked player for my age group. So it's either practice and pick up balls, or lose my matches. Tough work, easy choice! I want to stay on top."

He began to understand why she was so good at what she did.

"The program and process of becoming an On-Purpose Person makes a difference," she declared. "I will share with you that being the number-one ranked tennis player is not my top core want. There's more to my life than competitive tennis. My life has a wonderful balance in which tennis has a significant role. I have it in perspective.

"I'll leave you to your main draw," she concluded. "God bless you! Expect the best!"

He thanked her. He knew he had been in the presence of a special person. An On-Purpose Person—somebody who was achieving a long-term, extraordinary accomplishment—a true champion.

7

A NEW ORDER

▼

*Being entirely honest
with oneself is a good exercise.*

Dr. Sigmund Freud

Betty was right. The core want competition — choosing the core want in one area of his life over the core want in another account — had produced some "tough five-set matches." He had done it, though. He had completed the main draw.

As he looked over the results of his main draw, he realized that for the first time in his life he had order and clarity about what he really wanted. He had identified the single most important core want — a *number-one want*, the top one on his want list.

The beauty of having run the tournaments was that his wants were now placed in priority order. He had a tool for maintaining steady direction — a personal gyroscope amid the chaos of living his life. Now he could discern not only when he was *on-purpose*, but also when he was *off-purpose*.

His thoughts reached back to his boyhood, and a moment in which his father had said to him, "Son, at this time in my life if I were forced to make a choice, I would sooner be remembered as a good father than a good businessman." Now he finally understood what his father had meant. His father had made choices.

His father's priorities had acted as a tie breaker. Being a good father was more important for him than promoting his business career. *Wow, what a guy!* he thought, in a newfound understanding of and appreciation for his father.

A NEW WAY OF LOOKING AT SUCCESS

He knew that his father had made choices based upon personal priorities. Now *he* was free to choose whatever he wanted.

He reflected on his main draw. A tie breaker—
what a concept! He thought of how many times he
had been faced with a dilemma between two choices.
With a number-one want and other core wants clearly
identified, he had a benchmark—a point of reference
for comparing his choices. Previously, he had made
decisions "by the seat of his pants"—often based
upon a short-term outcome despite the longer-term
consequences. Finally, he had a foundation for making moment-by-moment decisions—a tie breaker.

It began to dawn on him that *he had created his
own definition of success*. For the first time in his
life, he had a clear vision of his wants and dreams.
So this is what an On-Purpose Person is all about,
he thought.

BUT WAIT—THERE'S MORE

Ring . . . ring. . . . The telephone broke in on his
musings.

"Hello?" he said, shaking off his reverie to focus
on the voice at the other end.

"Hello. This is the professor."

"Professor, what a pleasant surprise! Thank you
so much for all I've learned. It has *really* helped."

"I'm very happy to hear that, and you're welcome.
That, however, is not the purpose of my call.

"It's very important that you understand your
wants are not your purpose," the professor continued. "Purpose has a larger meaning that touches
all aspects of our lives. Your wants may give you
strong clues and insights to your purpose as it is
to be lived out today and for the future."

"Yes, professor. I'll keep my mind open to seeing a bigger picture than simply my wants."

"Great. I also called to remind you there are more people to visit. You're only halfway through the program. Keep going. Make your next call."

"Yes, sir! Right away."

I wonder what will happen now? he thought. Eagerly, he picked up his list to find the next name.

Step Two: The Plan

8

EFFECTIVE AND EFFICIENT

▼

The time which we have at our disposal every day is elastic; the passions that we feel expand it, those that we inspire contract it, and habit fills what remains.

Marcel Proust (1871–1922)

A s he approached the house of the third person on the professor's list, the man said to himself, "This is fun. I've met some fascinating people, each of whom is an On-Purpose Person. They really are a stimulating assortment of people. Their lives have meaning, yet their joy and excitement is built on a base of being comfortable and in touch with who they are, rather than on the basis of their possessions, status, or what other people think of them. They seem to be genuinely at peace with themselves."

EFFECTIVE AND EFFICIENT

It was a modest house in the suburbs, and definitely a home with children: He noticed toys on the front sidewalk and a swing set in the back yard. Its neat, well-attended appearance radiated a sense of warmth—whoever lived inside had carefully added the little touches that make the difference between a house and a home.

As he knocked on the door he waited expectantly to meet another new friend—another one of these On-Purpose Persons.

A trim woman in her thirties, wearing jeans and a sweatshirt, answered his knock. "Come in!" she said as she opened the door. "Let me introduce you to my neighbor Susan." They exchanged greetings.

"Susan's an On-Purpose Person, too. In fact, we meet each week to share our progress. I invited her here so she could meet you. She's going to sew new curtains for me and needs to measure the window openings.

"Please have a seat."

"Thank you for inviting me to your home. It looks like you have children?" the man inquired.

"I have a daughter and a son," she answered. "They are taking a nap—I hope. I understand you are well on your way to becoming an On-Purpose Person."

"That's right," he asserted. "I'm in creation. I've established my core wants and my number-one want. Now that I have clarity, I want to go out and start working on them. The professor called and reminded me to stay on-purpose, saying something about a bigger picture, so here I am."

"Oh! I understand your enthusiasm to get going. Be patient, though. By the way, what's your plan for being on-purpose?"

"My plan? Well, I guess I'm going to start with my number-one want and work on it as long as I can, then go on to the next, and so on and so forth. That's the way I learned to work through a list."

She smiled and asked, "Do you think that approach is practical, effective, and efficient?"

"I know it's efficient," he answered, "and I assume it will be effective because then I'll be working on my core wants. Anyway, what's the difference?"

"*Efficient* is doing things right," she replied. "*Effective* is doing the right things. On-Purpose Persons do things efficiently *and* effectively. That way, we have time to be on-purpose and off-purpose—because being off-purpose is bound to happen."

She continued, "Mastering time is essential to being an On-Purpose Person. That's why we each strive to do the right things and to do things right—efficiently."

"So when I'm on-purpose I'm being effective?" he asked.

"That's right!" she affirmed. "And when you are on-purpose . . ."

". . . I need to be efficient!" he finished.

She smiled. "You've got it!"

"That's great," he commented, "but my life is full of interruptions that knock me off-purpose. Sometimes I start my day with three tasks — only three! Yet, somehow I get off on a tangent. How can I stop that?"

She laughed and said, "As a mother of two little ones, I know about interruptions. From one perspective, their interruptions are disruptive. But from my on-purpose perspective, those supposed interruptions are consistent with my being a good mother, which is one of my core wants. I judge quickly what's really important to me because I have a tie breaker to guide me. Those interruptions become an opportunity for me to be on-purpose."

He could understand what she meant, but it wasn't hitting home yet.

"To answer your question, though — " she went on, "first, it's critical to have an awareness of being on-purpose or off-purpose. That's why On-Purpose Persons have the *light switch* as an anchoring device. Every time I use the light switch, it's a reminder to check whether I'm off- or on-purpose. When I measure myself, I see plenty of room for improvement. In baseball terms, I'm striving to improve my *batting average* — the percentage of the time I'm on-purpose."

He picked up on the new imagery. "What exactly do you mean by batting average?" he asked.

"Well, we're all On-Purpose Persons in creation. At times we're consistent with our purpose; other times we're not," she explained. "When we measure our activity and thoughts for a day and compare them to our purpose, what percentage of our day is consistent with our purpose? That's what we commonly refer to as our batting average."

She went on, "To stay on-purpose we must persevere with what is most important at the appropriate time. It requires strong-willed determination, assertiveness to state our needs, and good judgment. A purpose fortifies these qualities."

The man nodded emphatically as he furiously scribbled notes on a pad, trying to keep up with everything she was saying.

"If you keep your core wants in mind," the woman continued, "you'll develop greater sensitivity to changing situations and priorities. For example, my talking with you is on-purpose. If, however, one of my children falls out of bed and starts to cry, my priority shifts immediately to the child."

She paused and then started in on a new idea. "The second tool I have is the Ideal On-Purpose Day—" As if on cue, a child's cry sounded from another room. The woman excused herself to go check on her youngster.

He took advantage of the break to contemplate his personal on-purpose batting average.

How could he improve it?

9

THE IDEAL ON-PURPOSE DAY

▼

For mem'ry has painted
this perfect day
With colors that never fade,
And we find at the end
of a perfect day
The soul of a friend
we've made.

Carrie Jacobs Bond

The man sat waiting while the woman was comforting her small child. He had been learning about being effective and efficient as an On-Purpose Person. His batting average was low—even by Little League standards.

The Ideal On-Purpose Day the woman had spoken of earlier was new to him, or at least he hadn't heard any other On-Purpose Person mention it.

Just then the woman rejoined him.

"What do you mean by the Ideal On-Purpose Day?" he queried.

"If you don't mind," she said, "please allow me to ask you a question first."

"Sure," he responded.

"Do you feel your life is in balance? Or, in On-Purpose Person terms, are you balancing your accounts effectively and efficiently?"

Rolling her question over in his mind, he realized that imbalance was a large part of his frustration. He attributed part of it to not being in touch with his real wants—not doing the right things. He was off-purpose and unproductive.

Another area of his frustration was that when he was concentrating on one aspect of his life, the other accounts suffered and often a crisis arose. He went from crisis to crisis, putting out fires, never really doing what he wanted.

"I'm definitely not in balance," he finally answered.

"You will be in better balance once you apply the principles of the Ideal On-Purpose Day to your accounts. In my responsibilities as a wife, a mother, a scout leader, a Sunday school teacher, a part-time secretary, and more, my life is constantly in danger of being out of balance. I think most people working outside the home have it easy. At least they go to work for eight hours a day and focus on one aspect of their life over a prolonged, relatively uninterrupted time frame. I don't have that luxury. When I learned about the Ideal On-Purpose Day, it didn't change my circumstances: it changed my *response* to my circumstances. Now *that's* important!"

"I'm sold! Now please tell me—what *is* the Ideal On-Purpose Day?" he entreated.

THE TIME BUDGET

"Let's go through the Ideal On-Purpose Day step by step," she began. "The objective is to create a time budget, much like a person creates a financial budget."

He started taking notes again, so later he would have a record of the Ideal On-Purpose Day.

Continuing, she said, "First, draw a line down the middle of a piece of paper. On the left side, copy the headings from your want list. On the right side, write *Hours*."

"Okay, I've done that," the man stated.

"Now allocate time to each heading by hours or by percentage of a day. For example, you might designate eight hours or 33 percent of your time for work."

"I wish," the man said, exasperated. "I work very long hours."

"That's the point of this: Are you putting your time into the truly important wants and accounts of your life? Or are you unwittingly stealing from yourself, your family, or your employer?" she questioned.

"Create your time budget in a broad sense. Don't get hung up on details. Allocate your hours again and again until it feels exactly right. Here's a blank sample." She handed him a piece of paper. She left him to work on his time budget, while she helped her neighbor measure the windows.

THE 24 HOUR DAY	
Account	Hours or %
Physical/Health/Recreational Material/Financial Family Vocational/Career Social/Community Spiritual Mental/Intellectual Other	

BUILDING THE IDEAL ON-PURPOSE DAY

The man looked up and said, "I'm finished."

"Great! Next convert your budget into the Ideal On-Purpose Day. Across a clean sheet of paper write 'An Ideal On-Purpose Day.' On the first line, write the time you want to get up and on the last line write the time you want to go to bed. Between these times, fill in the time slots for the remainder of the day in quarter-hour or half-hour increments—whatever works best for you."

"Okay," he responded.

"Based on your time budget, begin filling in your time slots with the various accounts (vocational, family, spiritual, etc.). It may take you several tries to get your Ideal On-Purpose Day just right."

He began writing. After a few minutes he once again informed her, "I'm finished."

"What do you think you should do next?" she asked him.

"I should probably fill my schedule with the things most important to me—my most important wants."

"That's right!" she beamed.

He entered his most important wants next to their respective accounts. It made sense to him that if he was going to be on-purpose he must be sure about his wants.

When he finished he said, "Wow, that's simple. I don't know why I never did this before."

"Isn't that the truth! The beauty of the On-Purpose Person Program is its simplicity. Let's go on. By your response, apparently your Ideal On-Purpose Day feels meaningful."

"It does. Of course, in the real world I could never live up to this—with interruptions, emergencies, etc."

"You're right again. It is an *ideal day*, not necessarily a realistic day. The fact is, matters arise that distract us from the important wants. We must keep a diligent watch on our time and activity to be on-purpose. Otherwise, we're susceptible to being pulled off-purpose."

"Are we ever," the man agreed emphatically. "Can I have more than one Ideal On-Purpose Day—perhaps, one for work days, another for days off?"

"That's a good point. First, it is important to create an Ideal On-Purpose Day to have a sense of rhythm that best paces you. Once you have that, then there are all sorts of ways to use this tool."

"For example?" the man asked.

"For work days and for days off, as you suggested. My friend Susan, whom you met earlier, used the Ideal On-Purpose Day process with her husband to create their Ideal On-Purpose Vacation Day. Periodically, they give each other an ideal day as a gift. It's a neat idea, isn't it? My husband and I tried it and had a blast. Every so often we give our kids an ideal day. In essence, we honor each other on those days."

The man smiled. "That's a great suggestion. I think I'll do that with my wife and children."

"Do you have any questions?" the woman asked.

"Yes. Do On-Purpose Persons ever relax? It seems that this scheduling could get rather compulsive."

"Certainly we relax. Time for rest and recreation is essential. So much so that we schedule it into our day. How much relaxation time do you have now?"

"Not much, really."

"You see my point then," she said. "The Ideal On-Purpose Day is meant to be freeing, not constraining. We need to take care of ourselves—otherwise we're off-purpose. A symptom of not enough relaxation is getting sick. Sometimes a cold or the flu forces us to slow down. It can get to the point where we have a heart attack, breakdown, or depression. Our bodies can't be fooled for long."

The man said, "This can be very practical. My Ideal On-Purpose Day is the basis for a daily schedule. In essence, if I'm allocating my time to my most important wants on a daily basis, I can't help but be on-purpose and improve my batting average."

"I hope you become a batting champion."

His face brightened as he smiled. "Me too!"

10

TRUTHS

▼

If a man does not keep pace with his companions, perhaps it is because he hears a different drummer. Let him step to the music which he hears, however measured or far away.

Henry David Thoreau

The man arrived at the restaurant early. His next meeting was with Perry, a retired business executive who did freelance consulting. A gentleman approached his table. He was dressed in gray pants and a blue blazer with a smart-looking red tie set against a white shirt.

"Hello. My name is Perry James. I've been looking forward to meeting with you."

The man extended his hand in greeting as he introduced himself. They shook hands.

They made some small talk before ordering their lunches. The more time they spent together the more excited the man became. The conversation grew more personal. They shared their life stories with one another. A rapport developed quickly with Perry. It was as if they had known one another for years.

Perry brought the conversation to the matter at hand: "I have a unique perspective on the process of becoming an On-Purpose Person."

"I'm looking forward to hearing all about it," said the man. "Tell me more."

"What do you think is our greatest challenge and our greatest fear?" asked Perry.

The man thought for a moment, then said, "I guess knowing that we have a purpose. That we're not simply a freak of nature or a random occurrence in outer space. I want to know that my life has significance."

"I think you're right about that," Perry agreed. "Aren't we first and foremost spiritual beings wanting to know that there's a reason why we're here?"

"Absolutely, Perry. It just doesn't make sense sometimes. Yet I'm here. That's reason enough, 'cause if I wasn't supposed to be here, I guess I wouldn't be."

"State it positively. Your life has meaning, no matter what your condition or situation. You have a special purpose that's as individual as your fingerprints. And it isn't too late to act on it."

The man was strengthened and inspired by these words. This message of hope was radically different from the world of Madison Avenue advertising that unendingly bombarded him with inadequacies. From the clothes he wore, to the car he drove, to the food he ate—it was never good enough. Yet, in the midst of it all, *he* was good enough. He felt hopeful.

Perry continued, "Since we each have a significant purpose, then, what do you think our biggest fear might be?"

"Um-m-m, I'm not sure. Could it be finding out we've used up our purpose for being here?"

"That's very close. The fear is obsolescence. The good news is: we can't be used up. Our unique contribution is needed as long as we're alive. Obsolescence can come only if we allow it. Continual personal learning and growth is the cornerstone to remaining a viable On-Purpose Person. Our purpose is permanent and ever evolving to newer challenges. It is lived out differently over the stages of our lives.

"My unique perspective is my age. Many people who are my age have bought the concept of retirement as a sentence to death—a time to rest on their past and to freeze in time their minds and lives. In fact, retirement is a highly productive stage for an On-Purpose Person. We're less constrained by outside influences—more independent than we've ever been. Our batting averages can increase dramatically."

"That is a unique perspective. Obsolescence can be overcome, though, can't it?" asked the man.

"Of course it can and is. The first place to start is discovering your purpose. Thereafter, move boldly in that direction. You won't become obsolete. You see we're always needed when we're on-purpose. This is one simple truth of being an On-Purpose Person."

"Are there other truths, Perry?" the man inquired.

"Certainly there are," Perry assured him.

The man motioned for Perry to continue.

"Discover what's important. Not simply what is pressing or feels good or seems important—I mean those activities that are compelling to your purpose. Then, do them. Intentionally invest more and more time in the truly important matters. It is so easy to get derailed. But, why waste time on the nonessentials?" The man nodded in agreement.

Perry then added, "Time is a perishable and finite resource. As I age, I realize the days remaining in my life are precious few. I have had prostate cancer. It was removed and arrested. I'm happy to say I have a normal life expectancy. My lesson was learned the hard way. Therefore, I'm intent on on-purpose behaviors and activity. Does this make sense so far?"

"It sure does. Tell me more," the man prodded.

"Do you believe that our minds hold one thought at a time? Yes, we move rapidly from thought to thought. Nevertheless, we are limited to concentrating on one thought at a time."

"I agree. You're touching on an area of weakness for me," the man added. "My attention span and concentration are short. I'm busy but so unproductive."

"Put your time into compartments. The Ideal

On-Purpose Day is your foundation. Since you can focus on just one thought at a time, only attempt to do one thing at a time. When another concern pops into your mind, jot it down on your calendar, give it a time, and forget it until its time comes. Be at peace knowing there's time allotted to deal with it later."

"Compartmentalizing my time would do that for me. Tell me, how do I avoid off-purpose activity?"

"Use the On-Purpose Person's symbol—the light switch turned on—as a reminder to be on-purpose. One never fully avoids off-purpose activity. No one is ever 100 percent on-purpose, nor should one expect to be. Remember, improving your batting average is the standard. Your awareness of being on-purpose or off-purpose is enhanced as a result of writing out your Ideal On-Purpose Day. When you find yourself being off-purpose, stop what you're doing. Get back on-purpose! Like a gyroscope, you'll gravitate more toward being on-purpose minute by minute."

The man rolled his eyes. "Oh, that light switch haunts me. The other evening I came home from work and wanted to watch the news. It's my routine. My youngest daughter was playing on the floor in front of me. My wife was making dinner. As I pushed the power button on the TV remote control, the light switch came to mind. Suddenly I thought, *Is this on-purpose?* Spending time with my daughter is more on-purpose than watching the news. I realized she'd go to bed in another hour. Why not sit on the floor and play a game with her? That's what I did. We had a ball together. That's a habit I want to develop. Later in the evening, I watched the news."

"That is a terrific example," Perry praised him.

"Would you say you're seeing the world from a different vantage point?"

"Absolutely! Knowing I have a purpose and being on-purpose has been an eye opener. I still get caught up in day-to-day busyness. Over time it seems costly."

Perry placed his hands together in front of his face, almost as if he were praying. He thought for a moment. Then with a slowed pace and a softer tone, he spoke: "You bring up a very important principle. Business people are fond of saying, 'Time is money.' Typically they're speaking of time as an expense or time wasted. Instead, an On-Purpose Person thinks of time as if it were to be invested."

"I'm not sure I follow you," the man interjected.

"Where should you invest your time?" Perry pressed.

"Oh, I see! I invest my time in on-purpose activities. They pay the highest interest rates."

"You're right!" Perry exclaimed. "There's a tremendous compounding effect of the seconds of our lives. Our time accumulates into minutes, hours, days, weeks, months, and years. That accumulation can be positive or negative. An analogy is interest earned or interest paid. When we are on-purpose, we're earning interest on our lives; when we're off-purpose, we're paying interest. The Ideal On-Purpose Day is a tool for wise investing."

The man frowned as he spoke: "I don't think I can keep up with all the stuff that goes along with being on-purpose. There are want lists, tournaments, Ideal On-Purpose Days . . . it seems so programmed. Don't On-Purpose Persons ever let up?"

Perry let out a laugh. "I know it seems overwhelming now. But those tools are not meant to create a regimented, inflexible, compulsive plan. Quite the contrary. Put to appropriate use, they allow spontaneity, flexibility, and freedom. That's not to say you won't be called to make tough choices and sacrifices. Being on-purpose isn't always fun. The bottom line is this: It provides time for what is important to your purpose. Off-purpose activity is tiring and time consuming. Being on-purpose is energizing and fulfilling. It's just plain refreshing to be on-purpose.

"Going back to the time and money analogy," Perry recounted, "have you ever felt bankrupt in an area of your life?"

"Oh, definitely," the man confessed. "That's why I contacted the professor. My life was unmanageable. I was living on the edge of disaster physically and financially. My marriage was really suffering. The way I was headed, I couldn't keep it together any longer."

Perry picked up the conversation. "We must fiercely guard our life accounts and be aware when one is near empty. For example, I need exercise. I've had days when I knew I needed my workout to feel right. I monitor my time. I've found from week to week when my time averages close to my Ideal On-Purpose Day, I've had a good week. When I miss the mark on a given day, I know I've missed it—and more importantly, I know by how much and in what part of my life. Now I have insight into my stress and why I feel out of balance. I'm able to align my day-to-day activity with my purpose."

"That makes perfect sense," the man agreed. "Earlier you spoke of choices. My problems stem from my inability to make decisions. Another part is that my range of choices is limited due to too many bad choices in the past."

"You bring up some great points, young man! Choice is power. On-Purpose Persons excel at choosing. Why do we excel?" Perry paused a moment. "As you may have already learned, we have a tool called *a tournament*. It can be used for any decision. We have clarity and order about what's important. Do you know how to simplify your life?"

"Tell me!" the man begged.

"Focus your efforts on your number-one want. Let go of everything else. In a sense one regains his life by pruning back to the single most important want."

"That's an oversimplification," the man argued.

"Yes, it probably could be. But in a desperate situation it really is not. Regardless, the number-one want is the cornerstone to rebuilding. As progress is made, other wants can be added. The point is this: We have to cut life into manageable chunks. Most of us are not ruthless enough to prune our activities to the core."

"I understand and agree with you there," the man affirmed. "Let me push this line of thinking further. Isn't pruning, as you describe it, irresponsible to those around you?"

"Good point! On-Purpose Persons are not irresponsible to themselves or to others. Renegotiating arrangements or delegating are a couple of ways to prune obligations. Be forthright about it."

"It's a delicate balancing act, isn't it, Perry?"

"It is. This manner of thinking and ordering our lives is intended to enhance our development. When we're taking responsibility for ourselves, ultimately those around us are better off. However, the time during the transition can be excruciatingly painful, because old patterns are being broken."

The man continued asking his series of questions: "Do On-Purpose Persons ever go off-purpose intentionally?"

"No," Perry stated flatly. "Being in balance and on-purpose are distinctly different. From time to time, On-Purpose Persons may choose to be out of balance. Perhaps there's a major project that's essential to our purpose—then we go out of balance on a temporary basis. Giving ourselves consent to be off-balance tempers the ideal with the real—life, after all, has surprises. A few words of caution are appropriate: Constant out-of-balance activity leads to being off-purpose."

The man added, "As I look at my situation prior to learning about On-Purpose Persons I was, first, without a sense of purpose. As a result, I was way out of balance. At times the combination of no purpose and no balance felt overwhelming and scary."

"That's why," Perry resumed, "discovering one's purpose is the first step. Awareness of our purpose and the appropriate mix, or balance, of our life accounts is the essence of being on-purpose. This breaks the pattern of off-purpose and out-of-balance activity. Our accounts may become overdrawn if we fail to make compensating time, thought, and energy 'deposits.' We need to be aware of our trade-offs. For example, high stress, drinking, or a heart attack can all be indications of an overdrawn account. Being out of balance may limit our choices. Sometimes this disability to choose is temporary. Our choices can be permanently diminished as in the case of a crippling heart attack. In essence, a lifestyle, as we knew it, has died."

The man was amazed at this wisdom. Perry's statements were ideas he had already heard. The difference was he had never heard them related to his purpose.

Their conversation yielded simple guideposts to assist him in being on-purpose. Naturally he would be off-purpose from time to time. Like most people, he tended to default to the line of least resistance. Now he had some triggering and anchoring techniques to get back on-purpose and face the hard choices related to his purpose. He understood the causes for his frustration and uneasiness about wasted time. It was the result of being off-purpose. Armed with a purpose, new tools, and a plan, he had fortified his defenses to resist his natural off-purpose self.

Perry looked into his eyes. He sensed the man's feelings . . . the excitement, the sense of purpose, the anticipation of living day-by-day a newer, more fulfilled life — his determination never to be obsolete.

"My friend," Perry said, "before you leave, a word of encouragement: Set up your next meeting. It's an important one."

The man appreciated Perry. He was excited, challenged, renewed, and inspired. He knew Perry was right — each of us is a spiritual being at our core. It felt as though an empty hole in his soul was slowly being filled.

He was truly an On-Purpose Person in creation.

$$\boxed{11}$$

ON-PURPOSE STATEMENTS

▼

The first principle of ethical power is Purpose. . . . By purpose, I mean your objective or intention — something toward which you are always striving. Purpose is something bigger. It is the picture you have of yourself — the kind of person you want to be or the kind of life you want to lead.

Kenneth Blanchard and Norman Vincent Peale
The Power of Ethical Management

The man approached the red brick building. Flowers bloomed along the walkway leading to the entry door, which was adorned with a brass plaque engraved with "R. D. Scott Company." He turned the doorknob, entered the building, and stepped onto an exquisitely polished wood floor. *This place is impressive,* he thought.

"You must be Mr. Scott's nine-forty-five appointment," the receptionist greeted him brightly. "I'll let him know you're here. Please go down the hallway to the right. His assistant, Helen, will escort you directly to Mr. Scott's office. He's expecting you."

The hallway was lined with framed displays of all types—industry achievements and prizes, community service awards, and letters of commendation from customers.

An energetic, petite, comely woman with shortly cropped hair and well-tailored clothing extended her hand to him. "Hello, my name is Helen. We spoke yesterday when you called to arrange the appointment. I'll show you to Mr. Scott's office. He's looking forward to seeing you."

He was impressed. *What an organization—what people! They all seem to know their purpose,* he thought.

THE BENEFITS OF PURPOSE STATEMENTS

A tall, handsome man with graying hair framing a boyish face approached him, flashed a friendly smile, and firmly shook his hand. "Please call me Bob. I understand you've made substantial progress in your endeavor to become an On-Purpose Person?"

"Yes, Bob, you're correct. I've had quite an eye-opening experience so far," he answered.

"That's exciting! Please, have a seat. We'll get started. You've completed the first two steps—*a new beginning* and *the plan*. Now it's time to culminate your effort and insights in a workable set of guiding principles. The next step in the process of becoming an On-Purpose Person is an outward step. It's converting your energy in the self-discovery process into your On-Purpose Person Statements for interacting with the world—out there," he said, pointing toward the window. "It's a strengthening and clarifying process."

"How will I do that?" the man questioned.

"You'll be writing your Purpose Statements based, in part, on the prior steps," Bob explained. "Notice, I said statements—plural. Your Purpose Statements consist of statements of purpose, mission, philosophy, vision, commitments, and want list. Each statement is a different facet on the jewel called your life. Same jewel, different perspective."

The man interjected, "I've often heard people talk about mission statements, vision statements, and now, purpose statements. Even goals and objectives get mixed in there. They all sound the same to me. Please tell me the difference between them."

"You're right. Many people, particularly those in business, interchange the terms *mission, purpose, vision,* and *goals*. On-Purpose Persons have specific meanings for these. Purpose is a permanent, common thread woven throughout and in all parts of our lives. It exists in our past, present, and future. Vision, on the other hand, is future based. It inspires because it paints a visual picture toward where one is going by being on-purpose. Mission is directed outward and deals with the matter at hand in the present."

"That helps," the man commented. "What about goals?"

"Goals are consumable," Bob stated. "They add up. They're milestones along the way.

"Would running through a more detailed explanation of each statement be helpful?"

"It sure would," the man welcomed.

"Each statement is the outcome or response to a companion question. They're the newspaper reporter's tried and true questions of why, how, where, what, and who.

"First, your Purpose Statement is the spark. It requires rubbing two objects together. One of the objects has the potential to ignite and be transformed—that's us. The other object is relatively unalterable—the world around us. In other words, *to be living out our purpose we must be in contact with the world around us.* A Purpose Statement reflects what is within and what is outside of ourselves in relationship to each other."

"How do you write a good Purpose Statement?" the man asked.

"Answer the question, *Why do I exist?* and you have your Purpose Statement. It's an easy question to ask, but a demanding one to answer. We're searching for the meaning of our lives, given our unique experiences, talents, and potential. Expect to ponder this question for some time. It's a lifetime question. There's a spiritual dimension to purpose. At our core we are spiritual beings. The sooner we accept that reality, the sooner our lives become on-purpose."

"This is great!" he nodded. "Please go on."

"The Vision Statement is our projection into the future. It's a foretaste of something special to come. It's a *where* question — *Where am I going with my purpose?* Since purpose is the spark, then vision is the flame. It feeds the imagination, inspires the heart, and attracts others. Our vision is our dream and our hope. It sustains us during the inevitable trying times that come with choosing to live on-purpose. As a result, we bend, but we don't break. Yet our dreams alone are not enough. There must be more — a purpose that propels."

"A Vision Statement and Purpose Statement are closely related, aren't they?" the man asked.

"Definitely. In fact, a vision without a purpose anchoring it is most likely a costly diversion. Our Purpose Statement and our Vision Statement are related to each other but also distinct — and that's important to remember. The Vision Statement expresses our dreams. It's what we as well as others see. When writing our statements we're apt to jump to the Vision Statement and put off the Purpose Statement. Don't! A Purpose Statement is challenging to write. It disciplines us to answer a profound question that involves looking within. In comparison, the Vision Statement is exciting and creative. Can you see how a vision without the foundation of purpose is like a house built on sand?"

"Yes," the man replied. "You must be comparing it to the story of two houses, one built on sand and one built on rock. From all outward appearances the two houses appear identical. Both provide the same day-to-day comfort. The owner of the house built on sand may actually have more material comfort because his house with an inferior foundation cost less to build. But the other homeowner invested more to find bedrock. So he invested in peace of mind. When a storm arrives the house built on rock can withstand greater turbulence. I understand the analogy to mean that a vision with a purpose is far more capable of withstanding severe tests of resistance than a vision alone. It's true of the houses and true for our lives."

"Excellent example," Bob praised. "Purpose is a bedrock from which to build our lives.

"Let's go on. Mission is simply a specific and outwardly focused task we are doing. Your mission is a *how* question—*How am I to live out my purpose in regard to specific areas of my life today?* A space flight, a newly formed church, a sortie are all called missions. Mission gets confused with purpose because most of us repeat our missions over and over to become more efficient and effective. Therefore, we have a natural tendency to think our mission is our purpose. They're different."

The man nodded in understanding as he said, "The internal and external perspective and the element of time helps to distinguish purpose, mission, and vision from one another."

Bob up to this point had been sitting comfortably in a chair. He rose and walked to the window. He gestured with his hand toward the outdoors. "We have roles in which we live out our purpose. Our missions change, but our purpose is constant. You've met several On-Purpose Persons already. One is a high school student, a daughter, and a cheerleader. Another is a mother, a wife, and a part-time secretary. And then there's our friend the professor, who is a scholar, teacher, father, and husband."

"Excuse me, Bob," interjected the man. "My life roles are easy to identify. How do I turn them into missions?"

"Your roles are transformed into a mission when you recognize that they're the pathway through which you live out a greater purpose. Actors in a play have a specific role or mission in the performance. Our lives are very much like that. When we see the purpose behind our mission, we're more apt to excel in our role. Our purpose complements or matches our natural resources and gifts."

"You mentioned gifts. How do they fit in here?"

"Let's take an example. You met my receptionist when you arrived. She was hired and trained to do her job. That's the easy part. Identifying the gifts natural to the job and writing out the qualifications were the tough part. My employees are *gift-qualified*. New employees are trained in our systems as to the particulars of how we do things here. For example, I value friendliness in employees. I can neither teach nor legislate friendliness. Instead, I hired a naturally friendly person as our receptionist."

The man complimented, "I'm a businessman so I notice things about companies. You have a high-performance team here at the R. D. Scott Company."

"Thank you. We're an On-Purpose Business," Bob Scott said.

"What do you mean by that?" asked the man.

"We're very clear about the purpose of our company. We encourage each employee to become an On-Purpose Person. We don't try to change them, only to have them become more aware of their potential. It's a powerful and fulfilling linkage when the purpose of the individual is aligned with the purpose of the organization."

"Please tell me more about how to develop an On-Purpose Business," requested the man.

Bob held up his hand in a stopping motion. "Let's hold off the On-Purpose Business conversation until another day. For now, we need to finish talking about you and Purpose Statements. Weren't we just about to discuss the Philosophy Statement?"

"That's fair," said the man. "From what I gather, friendly and on-purpose are some of the traits here at your company. Are these part of your philosophy?"

"Correct," Bob confirmed. "Your Philosophy Statements answer the question, *What will be the manner or style for my conduct?* They're like the Ten Commandments of how you wish to lead your life. Here's where your personal ethics enter the picture. A sense of right and wrong is essential. Our society sets *minimum* standards. On-Purpose Persons set *high* standards and model them. We contemplate the issues and make our choices consistent with our Philosophy Statements.

"Your Commitment Statements are answers to the question, *What am I willing to do to achieve an item on my want list?* Look at your core wants and your Ideal On-Purpose Day. Can you commit to keeping them? These are commitments that you make to yourself and to others.

"Finally, there's your want list and the tournaments. Since you've already written out your want list, simply attach them to your On-Purpose Statements."

The man asked, "Can you give me an example of On-Purpose Statements?"

"Sure, I'll share some samples of my On-Purpose Statements with you," Bob responded. He reached for a folder from behind his desk, opened it, and began to read.

"Purpose Statement: I, Bob Scott, through love and service, encourage others to their potential.

"Vision Statement: To bring a smile, warmth, and encouragement to others.

"Mission: I perform my purpose as a husband, father, son, employer, community member, competitive golfer, and church member.

"Philosophy Statement: To model my purpose by dealing honestly, fairly, and with personal and professional integrity.

"Commitments: To be assertive and honest about stating my intentions and feelings.

"To leave Sundays free from my vocation in order to be with my family.

"To be open to suggestions and change.

"To deal honestly with my income taxes.

"To have zero tolerance for substance abuse in my environments and to maintain compassion for users by helping them find appropriate help.

"To provide a workplace where the people who come in touch with this company will be treated with extraordinary kindness and concern regardless of how bent out of shape they may be.

"To exercise with sustained aerobic activity for twenty minutes per day a minimum of four days per week.

"To live as closely as possible to my Ideal On-Purpose Day and to adjust my time to maintain my balance."

Bob looked up at him and asked, "Do you see how our Purpose Statement is the most inclusive statement? All the others build upon the bedrock of the Purpose Statement."

"Yes, I see how it all fits together," he answered. "Is it possible to have your purpose and your actual life really come together?"

"That's what integrity is all about," Bob responded. "As an On-Purpose Person you have clarified what's meaningful in your life. Now you have your *own* standards—not the standards of the world, your parents, your friends, or your enemies. You have created your own unique definition of success. It's yours and yours alone. When you live according to these standards, you have personal integrity."

Bob continued, "There's a woman who lives with the poor and sick, her income is minimal, and she has no possessions. By much of the world's standards of *material* success, she's a failure.

"Could anyone say that Mother Teresa is a woman without a purpose, a vision, a philosophy, and commitments? Yet that's the woman I just described—an On-Purpose Person functioning at a very high level."

"Wait a minute," the man interrupted. "I'm no Mother Teresa. She's a very high standard for you to present."

"Please don't misconstrue the example, my friend,"

the businessman warned. "In the nineteenth century, Phillip Brooks wrote in *Purpose and Use of Comfort*,

> 'Greatness after all, in spite of its name, appears to be not so much a certain size as a certain quality in human lives. It may be present in lives whose range is very small.'"

"In lives whose range is very small," the man echoed. "Wow, that is profound. It reminds me of a janitor I knew in college. He wasn't formally educated, yet what wisdom that man possessed. He was a positive influence on my life."

"That's another good illustration. It's helpful to translate these on-purpose principles into your own experiences.

"Quality is built into our lives by the smallest actions, attitudes, and behaviors. Improving one's batting average year after year — in other words, being more consistently on-purpose — is what's important. Perfection, or being on-purpose 100 percent of the time, is impossible. But a higher and higher batting average year after year is achievable. That leads to greatness."

The businessman continued, "Remember, think in terms of being on-purpose as a percentage. Ty Cobb was professional baseball's all-time leading hitter with a lifetime batting average of .367. That means nearly five out of every eight times at bat he made an out. That could be a very depressing statistic without the proper perspective. Like Ty Cobb, hold yourself to a high standard and keep a positive appreciation for what you have accomplished. With your new insight into purpose, your batting average will improve. Go for the long term—a slow and steady improvement. Perseverance and commitment are critical to being an On-Purpose Person over the long haul."

"My on-purpose batting average—it's a humbling statistic," the man gasped. "I imagine I'm on-purpose only occasionally, what with interruptions and responsibilities. It does give me comfort to know that being on-purpose is not a 100-percent or even a 50-percent issue. It's relative to where I am today and where I'll be tomorrow. Still, there are so many people who need me—in fact, count on me. I don't have that kind of control over my life."

"Sounds to me as though you choose not to exercise the influence you have," Bob said. "The whole point is to be intentional about your life, your purpose, your time, and your choices—day in and day out.

"Please be patient with yourself. Thinking in terms of being on-purpose is a tool to help you. If you turn it against yourself, you might feel guilty, depressed, or inadequate. Those may be genuine feelings, yet being on-purpose is a means to focus on what you *can* do, not on what you're *not* doing.

"Now, take a few minutes to contemplate your Purpose Statements. Then jot down your thoughts. There's no need to be profound. Keep them short and simple. You have a lifetime to refine them—that's why we say we're *in creation*. Start the first draft of your On-Purpose Statements right now.

"Please make yourself comfortable here in my office. I'll be back in thirty minutes. Take some time to think about and write down your statements. Write them now!"

90

IN CREATION

When Bob Scott returned thirty minutes later, the man started right in. "They're awful. My Purpose Statements are inadequate, incomplete. They're just—"

"Stop!" Bob commanded sharply. "They're written, and *that's good*. That's your start. Perfecting them is a lifetime challenge. Do you realize that very few people in the world have written Purpose Statements? Most organizations haven't even written Purpose Statements. You're special already. Remember, these Statements *evolve*."

"Thanks, I'll try to keep that in mind. But right now, I feel stuck here," countered the man.

"That's normal," Bob assured him. "Remember this is meant to be a freeing process. Some frustration is natural. When you're stuck, take action on your core wants. Be expectant and exploring. As you move boldly in the direction of your wants, your purpose will emerge in time. Keep looking for it and you'll find it.

"Now that your Purpose Statements are written, they'll be on your mind. You'll turn them over in your mind, attempting to refine and improve them. As this reflection continues, they'll take shape and meaning as you get closer and closer to your true purpose. That's part of what it means to be in creation. We're never through: The process is ongoing, our lives are developing. From time to time our Purpose Statements need to be revised, and perhaps updated. Remember, our purpose is within us and permanent. It will take time to unearth it."

"Okay, that helps," confessed the man. "It's all so new, in some ways—I wonder if I can really absorb it all and put it into practice. But I'll take each step as it comes — as you said, it's a lifelong process."

"Good — keep that perspective," Bob affirmed. "Come on — why don't you stretch your legs and take a brief break? When we come back, I'll go over one more important perspective with you."

12

THE SEASONS OF LIFE

▼

*We can define "purpose" in several ways.
For one, when we know our purpose, we
have an anchor—a device of the mind
to provide some stability, to keep
the surprises of a creative universe
from tossing us to and fro, from inflicting
constant seasickness on us. Or we can think
of our purpose as being a master nautical
chart marking shoals and rocks, sandbars,
and derelicts, something to guide us
and keep us on course. Perhaps the most
profound thing we can say about being "on
purpose" is that when that is our status,
our condition, and our comfort, we find
our lives have meaning, and when we
are "off purpose," we are confused
about meanings and motives.*

Dudley Lynch and Paul L. Kordis
*Strategy of the Dolphin:
Scoring a Win in a Chaotic World*

When the two men returned to the office, Bob Scott continued sharing. "There's a bigger picture of perspective to our lives that we often forget or may not even realize is present."

"What do you mean?" asked the man.

"Our lives have seasons and cycles that influence us," he began. "As you become more practiced at living on-purpose, you'll become more conscious of the seasons in your life and how to work *with* them rather than *against* them."

"Seasons and cycles in my life? Again I'm not sure I understand. You must think I'm not very smart, since I keep asking all these questions."

"On the contrary, I think your openness and desire to know and learn are positive signs."

Bob handed him a piece of paper. "In the 1970s a rock group recorded a song based on this passage from the Bible." He continued, "It's a great tool for giving me a bigger perspective—helping me realize that maybe I don't have as much control in my life as I may think I do. The passage is from the Old Testament. Please read this."

To everything there is a season,
A time for every purpose under heaven:

A time to be born,
    And a time to die;
A time to plant,
    And a time to pluck up what is planted;
A time to kill,
    And a time to heal;
A time to break down,

And a time to build up;
A time to weep,
   And a time to laugh;
A time to mourn,
   And a time to dance;
A time to cast away stones,
   And a time to gather stones;
A time to embrace,
   And a time to refrain from embracing;
A time to gain,
   And a time to lose;
A time to keep,
   And a time to throw away;
A time to tear,
   And a time to sew;
A time to keep silence,
   And a time to speak;
A time to love,
   And a time to hate;
A time of war,
   And a time of peace.
     (Ecclesiastes 3:1-8)

After reading the words the man looked up at Bob and said, "It gives me a bigger perspective—a larger context. I guess I was unaware of it. It helps me step back and see that I'm a part of God's creation, a small part of an enormous world. I remember being in an earthquake in California. I felt so minute, keenly aware of my limited sphere of control. It was humbling."

Bob smiled and commented, "That's a good analogy. On-Purpose Persons appreciate and are curious about the Creator, creation, and our purpose related to both. It's another reason why we're *in creation.* Here's another illustration.

"Imagine you're in a boat on a river. Some stretches of the river are smooth and quiet; other parts are turbulent and filled with rapids. Most of the river is an endless converging and mixing of currents and conditions that inevitably move you along. How do you react?

"People react as floaters, fighters, or navigators. Floaters passively resign themselves to accept the river in its present condition. They are the obsolete. They aimlessly go along for the ride."

"I know the type," the man quipped. "And they complain the whole time about how unfair the world is. Why they don't just take charge of their lives is beyond me. . . ."

"Now you're describing the fighters. They fight the forces of nature. These high achievers have victories from time to time. Yet they fail to realize how little control they possess. Inevitably the river's constant flow wears them down. They experience burnout, stress, depression, addiction, or many other manifestations of trying to control an indifferent river."

"Aren't we all really fighters or floaters to some degree?" asked the man.

"You're right. Whether we're naturally floaters or fighters isn't important. What is important is our ability to develop into navigators, i.e., to become On-Purpose Persons."

Bob's cadence quickened. "We On-Purpose Persons recognize we can't control the river. The best we can do is equip ourselves to navigate. We prepare and learn to read the river. We accept the givens and attempt to respond effectively and efficiently to the best of our ability."

The man suggested, "Perhaps that's how we got the expression *go with the flow*. Floaters are staying in the mainstream, rather than acknowledging the reality confronting them."

"That's probably where the expression originated," Bob answered. "On-Purpose Persons, however, adjust the expression to be, *Know the flow, then go with the flow*. We accept the river and its conditions. Yet we have not resigned ourselves to futile determinism — floaters. Nor have we foolishly tried to change nature's course — fighters."

The man asked, "What makes the difference for On-Purpose Persons, then?"

"The difference," Bob pointed out, "is knowing the river, equipping ourselves, and harnessing these resources to work with the river. How is your boat equipped? Do you maneuver in the water by using your hands, a paddle, an oar, or an engine? To navigate, do you have river maps, a guide, and experience, or only the seat of your pants? On-Purpose Persons don't have all of the equipment. We simply make the best of what resources we have available at the time. And we look for the means, methods, and resources to improve."

"Continuing personal development is what it sounds like to me," offered the man.

"It is exactly that," Bob confirmed. "The experiences and knowledge inside our minds can never be taken from us. These plus our talents and giftedness are especially suited for a special fit or purpose in this world. When times get tough, we navigate as best we can or we get a more experienced navigator to guide us. We know our lives have a needed purpose. We go toward the challenges with a perspective of expecting growth, development, and equipping. We succeed more frequently than before.

"The exploration you've experienced has been in three steps—*new beginning, the plan,* and *simplify.* You are now equipped as never before to harness the power of the river. You're already on your way: Now it's time for a reality check on your destination."

"What do you mean by my destination?" asked the man.

"The next On-Purpose Person will share more of that with you. Go in peace, with the newfound knowledge you possess. Discover, claim, and live your purpose. You have one."

They shook hands and parted. They were no longer strangers. They were bonded by their common journey along the path of discovery shared by On-Purpose Persons.

From out of the torrents in his life, clarity was emerging. The man knew he wasn't finished—after all, he was an On-Purpose Person in creation.

As the two men walked down the corridor, Bob patted the younger man on the shoulder. "I know this may seem overwhelming right now, but stick to it. You're on the right path. Good luck! Oh—don't forget to make that next call soon."

TRANSFORMATION

"It does not matter if you have been born in a duckyard, if only you come out of a swan's egg!"

The Ugly Duckling was so happy and in some way he was glad that he had experienced so much hardship and misery; for now he could fully appreciate his tremendous luck and the great beauty that greeted him.

. . . And he rustled his feathers, held his long neck high, and with deep emotion he said: "I never dreamt of so much happiness, when I was the Ugly Duckling!"

H. C. Anderson
The Ugly Duckling

| **13** |

CHOICES AND RISKS

▼

*Passion costs me too much
to bestow it on every trifle.*

Thomas Adams (1640)

The church bells rang out a familiar melody that the man remembered from his youth. *Amazing grace, how sweet the sound.* . . . He smiled and felt an inner warmth. It had been some time since he had set foot inside a church, except for weddings and funerals. He felt awkward about meeting this next On-Purpose Person—a clergyman. His thoughts kept gnawing the same bone: *I hope this minister doesn't try to convert or condemn me during this meeting.* He walked into the church office and asked to see John Harold.

Down the hallway came an average-sized, solidly built man wearing a brightly colored madras shirt. As he drew nearer, he extended his hand. "Hi, I'm John."

"Oh! Uh, hello," the young man stammered. "I was expecting—well, er—well, a minister—at least one with a black shirt and a white collar."

"I *am* a minister," John replied, his eyes twinkling as a smile spread across his face, "—I'm working undercover today."

They both laughed.

"Please, come down to my office," he motioned. The man followed him.

Once again the man was struck by the genuineness, warmth, humor, and quiet confidence these On-Purpose Persons had in common. Their lives were different, individually their own; yet their manner had much in common. They seemed to be navigating "the river" very differently from the rest of the world.

After a short walk down the hallway, they turned right and entered John's office. On one side of the large room was a neat desk with a huge bookcase behind it. Across the room were several comfortable-looking upholstered chairs and a couch.

As they sat facing one another in the cluster of chairs, a painting on the wall behind the minister caught the young man's eye. It was a depiction of Christ laughing. He had only seen pictures of Christ crucified, or those "sweet Jesus" holy portraits. This painting made Jesus look very human, very approachable. But the man still felt disturbed to be in a church.

PUTTING PURPOSE STATEMENTS TO THE TEST

"So what's the purpose of your visit?" asked the pastor.

"I'm seeking your assistance in hopes of becoming an On-Purpose Person," he answered. "I feel like I'm already a changed man. I'm hopeful you'll tell me more, please."

The clergyman grinned and spoke: "A reality check, that's what's left."

"A reality check? How do I do that?" he asked.

"It's simple. How does it feel?"

"Great!" was the reply. "I feel like a severely nearsighted person getting prescription lenses for the first time. There's clarity where there used to be a blur."

John pressed, "What difference do you think being an On-Purpose Person will make in your life?"

"It's going to be fantastic! Now I have vivid insight into my life's purpose, and I know my true needs will be met."

"I would like you to reexamine your Purpose Statements," the minister stated quietly, yet intently.

Uh-oh . . . thought the man, *here comes the conversion routine.* His uneasiness mounted despite the rapport he felt with the minister. In his most assertive manner, he asked, "Is this when you try to convert me?"

"No!" chuckled the minister. "I'll leave that to God's timing. Be open-minded about Christ. I encourage you to get to know Him.

"I can be open," the man conceded. "Go on, please."

"The purpose of this meeting is a reality check," repeated the pastor. "How strongly do you believe in your Purpose Statements? How worthy of you are they?"

"They're still fresh off the press, so to speak. They're coming along. I'm refining them," the man replied.

"My bottom-line question for you is–are you willing to lay down your life for your Purpose Statements?" asked the minister in a serious tone of voice.

"Probably not–uh, not yet, at least."

"That's okay," John assured him. "Remember that we're On-Purpose Persons in creation. When you believe in your Purpose Statements to the extent that you would suffer, even die, for them, then you will be richly blessed, for you will truly have found your purpose.

"A benefit of being an On-Purpose Person is your progress toward a worthwhile and meaningful destination. It's the journey where your day-to-day life is lived, and where discovery takes place. It's a series of milestones. Each day you make choices and take risks. You'll make mistakes—the wrong road—and you'll enjoy victories—milestones. In other words, you'll be off-purpose and on-purpose."

John's words had stunned the man into silence. If his life was to have meaning, he was going to have to face choices and risks consistent with his Purpose Statements. And maybe some of his choices would be emotionally severe, or even literally life-threatening. It was a scary thought.

He thought of the people who risked their lives in World War II, hiding Jews from the Nazis—they had risked everything for their beliefs. He remembered the striking news footage of a man who died after jumping into the icy Potomac River to rescue victims of a jetliner crash. He thought of the tragedy of an addict whose purpose, however off-purpose, is to get high—and so he risks it all, but without the opportunity for clearheaded choosing. He thought of his freedom as a citizen of the United States, and the lives of those who had died defending the rights that permitted that freedom.

He thought of a parent's love for a child . . . his own love for his children, and his willingness to die for them. Oh, how he had been shortchanging them. He realized then that his "dying" might involve some decisions about his job and his finances. It was still scary.

"John," the young man said softly, almost in a whisper, "I think I'm beginning to see how powerful purpose is. It exists at the very core of our being."

"Yes, it does," the minister answered Then he quietly left the room to allow the man a few minutes alone with his thoughts.

---━━━ **14** ━━━---

ON-PURPOSE
WITH PASSION

▼

*It is often simply from want
of the creative spirit
that we do not go to the full
extent of suffering. And the most
terrible reality brings us,
with our suffering,
the joy of a great discovery,
because it merely gives a new
and clear form to what we have
long been ruminating without
suspecting it.*

Marcel Proust

The minister returned to his office, where the man had been thinking for some time. His discomfort with the environment had been overcome by his discomfort about his choices.

"Tell me," John started, "what does the word *passion* mean to you?"

Blushing a little, the man answered, "I think of it as highly charged love or emotion, a burning desire—even to the point of being irrational."

Then he added, "Passion also brings to mind Tom Peters' book *A Passion for Excellence*. That's where he calls business people to a burning desire to excel."

"That's a pretty good definition," John responded. "But let's expand it from today's more popular usages to the seldom-referred-to first definition in Webster's Dictionary. It may shed new light on your purpose and Purpose Statements. It's important."

Going to the large bookcase behind his desk, the minister removed the dictionary and asked the man to read the first two definitions of passion:

"1. The Passion—the sufferings of Christ between the night of the Last Supper and his death. 2. Suffering. . . ."

As the man closed the dictionary, John continued, "Passion comes with purpose. It's the hard reality of living your Purpose Statements, the tough stuff of suffering.

"Let's look at Jesus Christ's life in human terms—the passion. He is the best example of an On-Purpose Person. He had a purpose he was willing to die for. His mission was the cross. His vision was salvation.

He suffered betrayal, denial by his friends, humiliation, beatings, spitting, torture, crucifixion, and ultimately death. Whether you believe in Jesus Christ or not, his life and teachings—as recorded in the Bible—are an excellent study about passion and purpose. Read about Jesus in the New Testament (Matthew 26–28). You'll learn that in going through the suffering of the cross there is another side—the resurrection."

John then added, "When you want to know about the purpose, the passion, and the impact Jesus Christ can have in your life, it would be my privilege to share his story. If not me, ask a follower of Jesus to share the story of his life."

The man had never heard of Jesus in such real, "un-church" terms before. He *would* read the Bible. Even though he considered himself an agnostic, he saw no harm in learning more. He knew enough to recognize a lesson to be learned on becoming an On-Purpose Person. He also decided that after reading the Scripture passages, he would reflect on his Purpose Statements and his passion. He would tie together his passion and his purpose.

In on-purpose terms, being on-purpose might not mean physical death, only "death" of a particular lifestyle or pattern. Death takes many forms. Perhaps it would mean quitting his job, or losing some financial security in order to fulfill his purpose. It could mean leaving an abusive relationship. Maybe it would mean more meaningful time with his family or other pursuits at the risk of career advancement. Or it could mean *more* emphasis on career. Perhaps it would mean less indulgence with food and drink.

These were disturbing thoughts.

Change is difficult, the man thought. *But the road I've been on is a sure and hopeless slow death. What choice do I have? I must choose life — life with a purpose.*

As he prepared to leave, the man extended his hand to the pastor — although it seemed a hollow gesture in contrast to the wisdom this man had just shared.

"I'd like to give you a hug," offered John. "May I?"

The man was startled by the request. He nodded his approval anyway.

John hugged him. At first the man's arms hung at his side as he stiffened in discomfort. Then, to his own surprise, he returned the embrace. Their hug was a genuine sign of mutual affection and esteem. It was comforting.

This was the first time he had hugged another man. Oh, how he wished he could hug his father! They didn't express love to each other with physical touch. Here was an opportunity for change — the next time he saw his dad he would risk it. He would give him a hug and see what happened. Whatever the outcome, he knew this was on-purpose.

Strangely, in his newfound openness, he felt a quiet confidence emerging. With each On-Purpose Person he met, he felt connected at a deeper spiritual level. These were very special relationships. He sensed that even in his brief and enjoyable journey of discovery and being on-purpose, somehow he was being transformed. He was becoming an On-Purpose Person.

15

THE ON-PURPOSE PERSON IN CREATION

▼

*The man who succeeds above
his fellows is the one
who early in life, clearly
discerns his object,
and towards that object
habitually directs his powers.
Even genius itself is but fine
observation strengthened by
fixity of purpose. Every man
who observes vigilantly
and resolves steadfastly
grows unconsciously into genius.*

Edward George Bulwer-Lytton
(1803–1873)

The man sat down in the chair in the professor's office. Several weeks had passed since his visit to see John, "the undercover minister." He had invested the intervening time in refining what he was learning. He had been anticipating this meeting with excitement.

"So tell me," the professor began, "how were your visits with the other On-Purpose Persons?"

"Professor, they were wonderful. I am an On-Purpose Person in creation. My life already has more meaning and balance. Everything is more worthwhile and fulfilling. I'm confident that as my skills in working the Program improve, my success and achievement will show it.

"I know there isn't less clutter in my life," he went on, "it just feels that way. I have a peace about me that I never had before. It hasn't been easy. I'm changing thoughts, habits, and relationships that were off-purpose. This is demanding and emotional work. Those old habits and life patterns are difficult to break. Because I'm trying to make changes in my life and others are not aware of it, it's easy to fall into old patterns with old friends. It's especially hard with my family. The patterns are like routines we get into unconsciously."

The professor nodded his head. "Go on," he encouraged.

"I remember being told that we train others how to treat us. Now that I'm observing the old patterns, I realize how destructive they were. They're off-purpose. Yet others seem to want to keep me in my old patterns. It's hard retraining them and myself as well."

"You're wise to be in touch with the changes you're making and the influence of the outside world," the professor commented. "I suggest you tell a few special people of the innovations and renovation you're engaged in. Ask for their support, encouragement, and accountablity."

"That sounds like a good suggestion, professor," the man concurred.

The professor continued, "Other than our choices, there is little we control. We are born with certain predisposed attributes and gifts, which we can discard or develop. They provide limitations as well as opportunities."

"Go on, professor. I'd like to hear more."

"The point is, we need to know who we are and what we can become. We each have God-given gifts, talents, and abilities that lead us in certain directions. Imagine trying to grow a tomato from a pumpkin seed—it's a ridiculous thought! The genetics of a pumpkin seed won't allow it to be anything but a pumpkin. Even then it needs good soil, water, sunlight, and nutrients to mature. The tomato has similar needs, but different genetic attributes. Yet how often we frustrate ourselves trying to be something we aren't."

The man added, "That ties in to the seasons and cycles of our lives, doesn't it?"

"Yes," the professor continued. "We all have incredible potential within, just waiting to be tapped. An On-Purpose Person accepts personal responsibility for discovering his or her unique attributes, and intentionally puts them to a positive purpose. I see students at this college chasing their parents' dreams for them to be a doctor or a lawyer or whatever. The problem arises when the students may or may not be gifted for the profession chosen for them by their parents. Other peoples' expectations can provide useful feedback. However, we need to exercise caution before we use them, if at all, to set the course of our lives."

"I understand, professor. What about timing? It seems to have a significant influence. Am I right?"

"Yes. The reading from Ecclesiastes that Bob Scott shared with you has special meaning for On-Purpose Persons. [See pages 94-95.] We realize that in the scheme of things, we're but a small part of God's creation. Our task is to find our purpose and then align ourselves with it—that is, to be on-purpose. There are many clues in our lifetime. We try to know the seasons of our lives. My seasons are different from your seasons. Once you accept responsibility for yourself, other people are powerless to impose their agendas and expectations on you. That is freedom and power. Freedom to choose, consistent with your purpose. That's not to say that your purpose may not be aligned with another person's purpose. It can be. Diligence to one's purpose is necessary in order to sort the on-purpose opportunities from the off-purpose alternatives."

"Professor, you and the other On-Purpose Persons have opened my eyes to the pattern of my life that at one time helped me succeed—pleasing others. Today, that pattern is a root cause of my failure, frustration, and disappointment. As an On-Purpose Person who accepts responsibility for my choices, will my life even out into smooth sailing from now on?"

"No, it won't be easy. Think about it. Is that what you really want? Without resistance, you can't build strength. You will continue to face challenges—only now you have new insight, new responses, and therefore new choices. I promise you, in many ways your life will be tougher. You are choosing a narrow, purpose-filled path. At times you will make seemingly unpopular, yet purposeful, choices. You will be different, and some people will take great joy in watching you falter or fail. Others will maliciously and deliberately try to pull you off-purpose. Don't give up. You must persevere."

"Does that really happen . . . other people pulling us off-purpose?" the man asked with amazement in his voice. He felt a flutter of anxiety.

The professor explained further, "I know of a young businessman whose choices led him away from a financially rewarding position because he found himself in an off-purpose situation. His ethics were challenged. His business associates were unable to understand that the basis of his choices was ethical and not financial. In worldly terms, his decision cost him financial hardship, yet he is at peace with the choice he made. His personal integrity and purpose are intact. More importantly, his personal convictions and values became more focused. His experience was grief-filled and grueling—but his response was positive."

The professor paused. He wanted his words to sink in.

"On-Purpose Persons see difficulties as opportunities from which to learn and to be strengthened," the professor continued, his voice gentle but firm.

"Pain is not something to avoid, but something to enter into with hope for growth and maturity. This long-term view of life is often our only saving grace in an unfair world. This is when passion is real.

"On-Purpose Persons seek their true successes in people, relationships, faith, love, and service — never in things. Ultimately, we are each responsible for defining our own standard for success. Some persons place it in dollars earned or possessions owned. Quite different people strive for a higher call. Their success is measured in terms of lives saved, minds taught, people served, and love given."

"Professor," said the man, "I see why being an On-Purpose Person is tough work. Being random about life is as easy as turning on the TV for mindless entertainment — it's just 'floating down the river.' Whatever happens, happens. It's purposeless — just letting life go by. On-Purpose Persons, on the other hand, expect, anticipate, and deal with distractions. That takes intention and attention. It's demanding to be on-purpose — to be a navigator."

"You're right. We avoid being random about our choices. We *choose* to be on-purpose." The professor added, "I have confidence that you are on your way to being an On-Purpose Person. Let's talk a little bit more about this. . . ."

16

GIVING

▼

We make a living by what we get, but we make a life by what we give.

Winston Churchhill

"Tell me more about what's changing for you," the professor probed.

"Well," the man began, "the time I committed to the On-Purpose Person Program is already producing benefits. I'm truly more content and less frantic. I'm operating more effectively and efficiently. It's also been a journey of self-discovery. As we talked about earlier, the On-Purpose Persons I've met along the way have shared insight into creation and my fit within it. I'm seeing a bigger perspective."

"That's terrific!" exclaimed the professor. "Believe it or not, you've experienced only the inside track of being an On-Purpose Person."

"Tell me, professor, if there's an inside track, then what's the outside track?" asked the man.

"Giving is the outside track. It's the other side of the coin that completes you as an On-Purpose Person. Without giving you'll eventually wither. Your time and effort in this process of becoming an On-Purpose Person have been a wise investment. Your focus and attention have been on self—on a discovery of self. Do you agree?"

"I agree."

The professor went on, "On-Purpose Persons are joyful, intentional, and proportional givers. Your On-Purpose Person Program is a solid foundation. Build on it. Now you have enhanced personal insight. You have a responsibility to put your purpose to good use for yourself, your family, and others. You have the basic building block of being a leader—a purpose."

"Professor," the man broke in, "it makes sense that I should be giving, but how do I start? What do

I have to give that's worth anything? Who should I give to? When do I have time to give?"

"You know the answer to some of those questions already," responded the professor. "I'll give you a hint: Start with a *give list*."

The man immediately picked up on the professor's hint and added, "Then I bet I run a couple of tournaments—like a qualifier and a main draw. And eventually I'll come up with my core givings. So I'm to cycle through the Program using a give list like I did with my want list?"

"Basically, that's correct," answered the professor. "As we discuss giving, you'll see how it's integrated within all On-Purpose Person living. For now, let's talk separately about joyful giving, intentional giving, and proportional giving. Finally, we'll pull them all together so you can be a joyful, intentional, and proportional On-Purpose Person giver."

"That sounds great, professor. Tell me—why do you call it *joyful* giving?"

"Giving out of joy and thanksgiving for our blessings is the building block for successful giving. You've had the opportunity for some intense self-discovery in the process of becoming an On-Purpose Person. You're more aware of the special gifts, talents, and resources you possess. You are uniquely qualified and blessed. There's no one else in the world exactly like you—you have a purpose. Someone or something needs you. For you to fulfill your purpose you have to serve others from your abundance.

"Meaninglessness in life stems from two primary causes: being off-purpose and not giving. You're well on your way to being on-purpose. Now, learn the lesson of joyful giving."

"Professor, I hear you and I understand. But it's hard for me to let go of what I've worked so hard to get."

"You're not alone. That's why giving must be *intentional*—in other words, a committed priority."

"How can I fit another priority into my life?"

"You don't *fit it*—you make giving the first activity. All else fits around your giving."

"Whoa, professor. Now there's a radical statement. You mean, I'm to turn my recently well-ordered and on-purpose life upside down, take my core wants and put them aside? Do you want me to be a third-world missionary or something? It's all made sense until now."

The professor laughed. He really admired the man's candor. "Please let me finish. Then ask your questions. Okay?"

The man nodded his agreement.

"Keep in mind that I said giving is joyful, intentional, and proportional. Let's talk about giving in proportion to our means."

PROPORTIONAL GIVING

"On-Purpose Persons have a minimum standard of giving," explained the professor. "We keep up to 90 percent of all we earn. In other words, we give a minimum 10 percent to others—that's giving in proportion to our means. My resources are different from yours. Our means are different from the means of an unemployed person or the chairman of a Fortune 500 company. One person's resources are no more or no less important than another's—just different. But our Madision Avenue society sells it differently. Think about the Program you've started. You've defined your terms for success.

"Abundance follows being on-purpose because we create value. Giving out of our abundance is natural. We measure ourselves in proportional terms, not in absolute terms. By the way, you don't have to be a missionary unless it's on-purpose for you.

"Thanks, that's a relief!" They both smiled. "You talk about our *means*—please be more specific, professor."

"Our means are our time, talents, and resources."

"Professor, how do I give of my time? My Ideal On-Purpose Day is already scheduled and keeps me on-purpose."

"Give first. Remember, you will determine your core givings just like you discovered your core wants. You can only allocate so much time to so many giving opportunities, so make them the most meaningful and on-purpose.

"There are just twenty-four hours in the day, so at 10 percent we give two hours and twenty-four minutes each and every day to others. That giving rarely occurs in two-hour-and-twenty-four-minute chunks. We can give of our time through volunteer opportunities as well as small spontaneous acts of kindness or courtesy. To demonstrate my point, I'll create an imaginary On-Purpose Day with giving.

"You get up, you exercise, you go to work, you come home, you eat, you go to bed. Pretty basic stuff, wouldn't you say?"

The man nodded in agreement.

"Here are your opportunities to give. Awaken five minutes early to hold and hug your wife. Tell her you love her as you arise from bed. While on your morning jog, greet neighbors and other joggers with a smile or friendly remark.

"Upon returning home, instead of dumping your sweaty clothes on the floor, put them in the washer along with a load of other clothes. Help one of the kids find her lost pencil—joyfully. On the way to taking the children to school, let someone cut in traffic ahead of you.

"At work, take five minutes to really listen to your assistant and ten more minutes to help her—joyfully—with something she doesn't understand. At noon, hold the door to the restaurant for the elderly man with a cane who's fifteen seconds behind you and, when he passes by, smile and greet him. If appropriate, touch him. People respond to smiles and touch.

"As you leave the office, compliment the janitor on a fine job of cleaning your office and let him know how much you appreciate what he does. Let another person or two in line during the rush hour traffic. Smile at them if you can. Be genuine in your giving."

"Professor, I've got the picture. You're right, it's basic courtesy and an awareness of the hundreds, if not thousands, of opportunities that present themselves day after day."

The professor continued, "Planned giving or volunteer opportunities abound. On-Purpose Persons allocate a portion of their giving time. I know of the giving by a burly On-Purpose Person who is a former NFL all-pro lineman. He's the head football coach here at this college. In the off-season he goes to a local hospital to hold, rock, and love newborn babies—babies who have drug-addicted moms. There's a volunteer opportunity for you in your church, in the government, or somewhere in the community."

"Giving of my talent is fairly easy to figure out, professor. May I tell you what I think it involves?"

"Please do," allowed the professor.

"My talents are my skills and abilities. For example, I'm an accomplished magician. I love it, but I don't have reason or time to practice my tricks. Perhaps I could go to the local children's hospital to entertain the kids. It would be fun. In fact, it was on my want list. Am I right, professor?"

"Yes. On-Purpose Persons see giving opportunities as ways to create win-win situations. Professionals such as lawyers, accountants, and consultants may give their expertise to those who can't afford their services, or to nonprofit organizations. Others see giving as an opportunity to do something totally different from their work—like the football coach. Many communities have volunteer service bureaus to match people to needs.

"Our talents need not be perfected, only available. It's important that we realize our talents exist. We tend to take for granted much of the giftedness we possess. We can hold someone's hand, so we can comfort. We can drive a car, so we can deliver food to shut-ins through an organization such as Meals on Wheels. We can read, so we can teach someone else to read, or we can read stories to children.

"Are you ready to talk about the resources you have to give, young man?" queried the professor.

"Yes, sir."

"Resources are both manmade and natural. Manmade resources are money and material possessions. Giving our time and talent is often one thing, but when we start reaching into our pocketbooks it can be quite difficult. Let me reaffirm the On-Purpose Person's giving standard: We joyfully and intentionally give 10 percent of our income. This means we keep a maximum of 90 percent of what we earn. Don't forget, the *first* 10 percent goes to others, not the last 10 percent. Otherwise, our giving becomes leftovers—or, more likely, it doesn't happen at all."

"You've got be kidding—*10 percent* of what I make goes to others? I'm leveraged to the hilt! That's unrealistic and arbitrary. There's no way," the man protested.

"Remember, giving involves tough choices and keeping priorities. The willingness to give away our possessions means they no longer possess us. In other words, our self-worth is not wrapped up in the size of a paycheck or house or the kind of car we drive. Material goods disappear as quickly as they appear, so why build a life on that sandy foundation?"

"Professor, once again I take issue with what you're saying," the man asserted respectfully. "That sounds like college rhetoric. There's a real world out there. I have to live in it."

The professor smiled, rubbed his chin, and sat back in his chair before speaking. "Your frankness is refreshing. Please, hear me out. Material goods are essential and needed. Let me pose it as a question: 'Do your possessions possess you, or do you possess them?' Being a materialist is ultimately a dead end."

"I agree, professor. All the things I've accumulated

really haven't brought me happiness. Still, it's hard to let them go."

"It's unrealistic for you to go 'cold turkey' without material goods. You may need to wean yourself gradually. It takes a purpose with a passion," advised the professor. "For example, could you and your wife develop a household budget that cut expenses and steadily increased giving, so that in five years you could be giving 10 percent?" asked the professor.

"I guess it's possible. We're probably giving about 2 percent of our income to charities and others now. If we cut a few luxuries and increased our giving another 2 percent each year for the next four years we could manage it," the man conceded.

"Great! Perhaps that's your plan. Maybe after your next annual review, your raise could go to giving. Giving is done joyfully out of our abundance and in thanksgiving for our blessings," reminded the professor. "It's an attitude of gratitude."

"Professor, I admit that you're right. In comparison to others, some are better off than I am, but most don't share my blessings. I am where I am—that's my starting point. This is a struggle for me. It's going to take planning and soul-searching."

"Wouldn't it be great if your children grew up free from the attitude of material accumulation as the basis of their self-esteem? You can help them. I suggest that you make giving a family project. Include your wife and children with selecting the areas of giving. Involve them in the financial planning. Then model it. Put your time and money into action. It will be an unforgettable lesson for your children."

"Absolutely! What a gift for my kids!"

NATURAL RESOURCES
AND INTERDEPENDENCE

The man picked up his line of questioning once more. "Tell me about our natural resources."

"In the biggest sense, our natural resources are our environment. In the most personal sense, our natural resources are our physical bodies.

"Our environment has replenishable resources. For example, trees absorb nutrients and light to produce life-giving oxygen; they drop their leaves and create more nutrients, and so goes the cycle. But cut off a limb, and it's gone.

"We're like that tree. If we lose a limb—a kidney or an eye—it's not replenished. Today, organ donors give life to another through transplant surgery. They respond to a need in a highly committed manner. They see life beyond themselves. It is an on-purpose act of giving.

"We also possess replenishable natural resources. Physically, blood and bone marrow are two examples. There are also natural resources we can impart to one another. A smile, a compliment, a hug, or a kiss are unlimited natural resources. So be generous."

The man nodded in agreement. "I never noticed how many ways there are we can give to one another. Is there a greatest giving of all?"

"Love in its many forms is the greatest gift of all," declared the professor. "It's a highly replenishable resource. The more you give, the more you receive. This is a simple principle that On-Purpose Persons attest to as the truth behind all giving."

"Professor, I see how interdependent we are on

one another. Giving of ourselves is an essential ingredient of being human. The image of the strong independent type is just hype. I know lots of men and women who are hurting down deep, but they maintain a self-sufficient image in fear of exposing themselves. I can see it on their faces, though—they're desperate. It shows in stress, overeating, over-drinking, addiction, affairs, or ill health. They're killing themselves. That's the way I was before I called you."

"Young man, you seem to have learned and embraced the On-Purpose Person concept of joyful, intentional, and proportional giving. Tomorrow we're scheduled for another meeting. Tonight, create your giving list. By the way, you'll find that part of your giving list is contained within your want list. It's gold waiting to be mined. Go over each life account and write down the wants that are really givings. Then add any new givings to your giving list. Next, run the tournaments to determine your core givings, and then organize your On-Purpose Day around your giving. Review your On-Purpose Statements for any changes you might want to incorporate."

"Whew! I'd better get going. This could take several hours," the man exclaimed.

"You're right! Instead of meeting in my office tomorrow, we'll meet in room 412, the conference room down the hall. I'll see you there tomorrow at six p.m."

17

THE GATHERING

▼

Union gives strength.

Aesop
The Bundle of Sticks (550 BC)

As the conference room door swung open, the man was surprised to find it occupied with all of the On-Purpose Persons he had met. They cheered and congratulated him.

The professor called out, "Welcome to your first On-Purpose Person Gathering. For short, we call it *Gathering*."

"What a pleasant surprise!" the man exclaimed. "Thank you all for your guidance in my process of becoming an On-Purpose Person. This is great."

After a few minutes of reunion everyone settled into chairs around a large wooden conference table. The professor began.

"On-Purpose Persons are in the vast minority. Many of us gather together once a week to review our respective progress, to encourage and support one another, and to have accountability. A Gathering can be two or more On-Purpose Persons. We call each other gathering partners. We combined groups for your *commencement*. Some On-Purpose Persons choose not to belong to a Gathering for whatever reason. I advocate Gatherings for the support, encouragement, and accountability they provide.

"We use a simple format to review our weekly progress, whether we're at a Gathering or not. Here's a *gathering agenda*. [See pages 139-142.]

"You'll notice the agenda is broken into sections— On-Purpose, Giving, and Transformation. At a minimum, Gathering is fifteen to twenty minutes long. That's up to the gathering members to determine."

The high school student said, "We begin each Gathering by reading aloud Ecclesiastes 3:1-2. Then we step back and view our lives from the bigger perspective of what season we're in today."

The homemaker added, "We review our Folders as reminders of our purpose."

Betty Rose spoke: "Next, we discuss how we've done as On-Purpose Persons that week by using the questions and comments provided as springboards for discussion. It isn't necessary to answer each question. They're just aids to jog our thoughts."

John, the minister, interjected, "The next item is giving. We make sure we haven't fallen victim to being too self-centered. The group is a safe haven to share concerns and joys, and to review and discuss our on-purpose successes and failures."

Bob Scott said, "It's also a time to give feedback, to hold one another accountable, and to encourage one another. We talk about our lives and any concerns we may have for the coming week."

"Relationships are built in the gathering partnership," Perry added. "That leads to friendship, which leads to openness, which leads to personal innovation and development, which leads to wisdom, which is all about having a purpose and being on-purpose."

"Finally," said the professor, "sharing transforms us into On-Purpose Persons. We look to share the Program with others. Who is ready and can benefit from being an On-Purpose Person? Sometimes the best we can do is plant a seed. An On-Purpose Person gave you my name some time ago. Eventually, when the time was right, you sought me out. You can't own it until you give it away to others. That's the On-Purpose Person's paradox."

The man smiled. "It amazes me. I start by writing

down all that I want, and I end up giving it away. It is a paradox."

The professor said, "My friend, what you're giving away is the Program—a process. Give it freely. Your purpose, if hoarded, would eventually wither and die. Instead, provide for it abundantly, and it will thrive, evolve, and transform you and others. That is the essence of the next stage—becoming an On-Purpose Leader."

"Professor, that's wise counsel. I will stay focused on discovering my purpose. I will align my life so that I will be on-purpose. I see that purpose is a cord woven through all my life accounts. Getting clarity about my purpose is my primary mission today."

Before departing the Gathering, the man made a point of talking to Perry, the consultant. Perry spotted him approaching. As they shook hands, Perry placed his left hand over their grasped hands. To the man, this demonstrated friendship. This was the reason why he especially wanted to talk with Perry—he already felt a close relationship with him.

He began, "Perry, our talk a while back made a strong impression on me. You did also. I want to get to know you better."

"I would like that," Perry agreed at once.

Encouraged by the response, he pressed onward. "I have a long way to mature in becoming an On-Purpose Person. Would you be my gathering partner?"

They had an in-depth discussion of their respective expectations and commitments. Gathering partnerships, Perry explained, are not one-way arrangements. As they continued to talk that evening they agreed to be gathering partners.

THE REWARD

We never know how high we are
Till we are called to rise
And then, if we are true to plan,
Our statures touch the skies.

Emily Dickinson

---- **18** ----

TRUE SUCCESS

▼

*We are here to be excited
from youth to old age,
to have an insatiable curiosity
about the world. . . .
We are also here to help others
by practicing a friendly attitude.
And every person
is born for a purpose.
Everyone has a God-given
potential, in essence,
built into them.
And if we are to live life
to its fullest,
we must realize that potential.*

Norman Vincent Peale

Years had passed since the man's first Gathering in that college conference room. Today he was known throughout his community as a man of extraordinary accomplishment, faith, and quality of character.

The Program was etched in his mind. He applied the principles and process with ever-increasing skill. He made decisions consistent with his purpose. Every year since that first year, he set aside two or three days to rework the Program. It was his cornerstone.

He and Perry had been weekly gathering partners for some time. Eventually, their circumstances changed and they were no longer able to meet. The man had shared the On-Purpose Person Program with his closest friend. They became gathering partners. In time they shared the Program with others and mentored them. As a result of the man's original gathering partnership with Perry branching and then those groups branching out again and again, literally hundreds of people experienced the Program. Gatherings were taking place at schools, churches, businesses, and homes. Thousands of lives were being touched, changed, and transformed as individuals were discovering their purpose and being on-purpose. They encouraged and cared for one another.

The man had shared the On-Purpose Person Program with his wife. She noticed the transformation in his life and in their marriage. She asked a friend to be her gathering partner. This partnership grew and branched out, giving birth to hundreds of new Gatherings.

Life was still not fair. The "river current" surprised him from time to time. He encountered rapids and whirlpools that threw him off-balance. These were times of transition, strengthening, and growth — an essential aspect of life. He maneuvered through them with his purpose and gathering partner as compass and crew, respectively.

The man's personal net worth had grown — and so had his financial net worth. His relationships with family, friends, business associates, and neighbors were positive, productive, and fulfilling.

He had prospered materially, eventually becoming the president of his company, but money and status no longer controlled his life. When he stopped chasing worldly success and reordered his life based on his purpose, his wants were plentifully met. He was living and giving abundantly.

Periodically, he would open and review his folder from that first year of the program. It amazed him how many of those wants he had either accomplished or acquired. Even more amazing was how his present wants were so much deeper and fuller than he could even have imagined back then. It was humbling to see the significance of his life as it was being used in the creation.

He truly was a man who, with the help of others, was living and creating a meaningful and balanced life, founded on his definition of success and achievement. The On-Purpose Person Program worked!

One afternoon, just minutes before leaving his office, his telephone rang. He picked up the receiver and heard a young man's voice: "Sir, I'm not quite sure why I'm calling you. I'm so confused. My life is torn in so many directions. I feel out of control. A friend said you are known as an On-Purpose Person. I would like to learn more about it. Would you be willing to share with me what it means and how I can make sense of my life?"

"Yes! I understand why you're calling," replied the man. His pulse quickened with excitement—an opportunity to enable another person to discover his purpose and to be on-purpose. An On-Purpose Person has the joy and the responsibility to pass along what others are giving to him. This is what it means to be an On-Purpose Person.

He had become an On-Purpose Person.

THE
ON-PURPOSE
PERSON
WEEKLY
GATHERING
AGENDA

Begin by reading the following passage aloud together:

> To everything there is a season,
> A time for every purpose under heaven:
>
> A time to be born,
> And a time to die;
> A time to plant,
> And a time to pluck up what is planted.
> (Ecclesiastes 3:1-2)

■ From Ecclesiastes, I identify the current "season" of my life as being a time to. . . . Why?

■ I do/don't see a change in season. . . .

ON-PURPOSE

Open your On-Purpose Folder, review, and read your On-Purpose Statements.

Next, within the Gathering openly respond to the appropriate questions.

■ I have most recently achieved these items on my want list. . . .

■ If I feel out of balance or off-purpose, I need to make these changes to be on-purpose. . . .

■ The recent day that was closest to an Ideal On-Purpose Day was. . . . Why?

■ The recent day that was furthest off-purpose was. . . . Why?

■ I made an intentional choice that moved me from off-purpose to on-purpose. It was. . . .

■ These impediments are preventing me from being on-purpose. . . .

■ I am doing this to remove them. . . .

■ My on-purpose batting average did/didn't improve. . . .

■ To prepare and equip myself for being on-purpose I have undertaken the following actions. . . .

■ I had . . . (state number) opportunities to review my On-Purpose Folder during the past week.

■ My most on-purpose moment was. . . . Why?

■ My most off-purpose moment was. . . . Why?

■ The following recent experiences tested the passion of my purpose. . . .

■ In the coming days I face the following challenges and opportunities to my being an On-Purpose Person. . . .

GIVING

■ I have/haven't given joyfully, intentionally, and proportionately according to my
means. . . .

■ I have/haven't given from all three areas —
time, talent, and resources. . . .

■ My giving has/hasn't been consistent with
my give list. . . .

TRANSFORMATION

■ I believe the following person would benefit
from knowing about the On-Purpose Person
Program. . . .

■ I shared or introduced the concepts of the
On-Purpose Person with this person. . . .

■ This will be my follow-up action. . . .

CONCLUSION

Each week read one quote from the beginning of a
chapter in *The On-Purpose Person*. Discuss it.

AUTHOR

Kevin W. McCarthy has dedicated his professional life to helping others be on-purpose, personally and in the organizations they serve. Toward fulfilling this commitment, Kevin has written two books and founded The Purpose College. He also speaks, trains and consults on the topic.

Kevin first read the book *I'm OK, You're OK* in 1968. It began a personal development journey with thousands of hours of reading, contemplating, searching, listening and discovering. The benefit of his searching culminated in *The On-Purpose Person* and *The On-Purpose Business*, his first and second books, respectively.

Kevin is the President of US Partners, a general management business consulting firm, and the Founder of The Purpose College. He is an accomplished speaker nationally and internationally and a member of the National Speakers Association.

A native of Pittsburgh, Pennsylvania, Kevin graduated from Shady Academy, Lehigh University, and The Darden School (the graduate business school of The University of Virginia). With his wife, Judith, they have two children, Charles and Anne. He is active in his church and community. His personal purpose statement is "Being On-Purpose!" Kevin's joy is inspiring others to turn on their "light switch" and be on-purpose!

THE PURPOSE COLLEGE RESOURCES FOR INDIVIDUALS AND ORGANIZATIONS

The Purpose College is dedicated to the development of resources for the training of on-purpose persons. *The On-Purpose Person* is the cornerstone. Kevin W. McCarthy's second book, *The On-Purpose Business*, helps on-purpose persons live out purpose where they work, volunteer, worship, gather and live. The Purpose College offers the following Programs:

- The On-Purpose Person™
- The On-Purpose Business™
- Generation Extraordinary™—an on-purpose program for teens and young adults

Are you:

- Interested in receiving a series of *free* articles about becoming an On-Purpose Person?
- Interested in participating in The On-Purpose Person Program?
- Feeling called to help others become On-Purpose Persons by becoming a "Professor?"
- Considering Kevin McCarthy or a Professor as a keynote speaker or workshop leader for your next meeting, retreat or convention?
- Wanting to share your story of how *The On-Purpose Person* has touched your life?
- Wanting to know of additional On-Purpose Resources?

If yes, then you're invited to contact The Purpose College at:

The Purpose College
P.O. Box 1568
Winter Park, FL 32790-1568
(407) 657-6000